WordPress Development in Depth

by Peter B. MacIntyre and Sávio Resende

WordPress Development in Depth

php[architect] edition published: August 2020

Print ISBN:	978-1-940111-83-4
PDF ISBN:	978-1-940111-84-1
ePub ISBN:	978-1-940111-85-8
Mobi ISBN	978-1-940111-86-5

Produced & Printed in the United States

Disclaimer

Written by
Peter B. MacIntyre and Sávio Resende

Managing Editor
Oscar Merida

Editor
Kara Ferguson

Layout
Oscar Merida

Published by
musketeers.me, LLC.
4627 University Dr
Fairfax, VA 22030 USA

240-348-5PHP (240-348-5747)
info@phparch.com
www.phparch.com

Table of Contents

Foreword

What you are about to read is a map, but it's the kind where you get to build your own roads.

One of the greatest joys in my life has been to discover some code, make it work for my needs, and then give it away. In this particular instance, the code I discovered was a blogging platform written in PHP called b2 / cafelog, developed by Michel Valdrighi. I had embraced it as a way to publish my thoughts and photographs on the web. As it happened, Michel had moved on to other projects, and I was left with the question of whether to fork b2 and build on top of it. I blogged about it at the time:

> *"Fortunately, b2/cafelog is GPL, which means that I could use the existing codebase to create a fork, integrating all the cool stuff that Michel would be working on right now if only he was around. The work would never be lost, as if I fell off the face of the planet a year from now, whatever code I made would be free to the world, and if someone else wanted to pick it up, they could. I've decided that this is the course of action I'd like to go in, now all I need is a name. What should it do?"*

With the help of another developer, Mike Little, we forked b2 and developed what became known as WordPress. That was 2003.

What you are about to read in this book is the result of millions of people, with millions of lines of code, doing the same thing I did back in 2003: Discovering something useful, manipulating it to fit their needs, and then paying it forward. It's the promise of open-source software, and you're now reading the instruction guide for 17 years of evolution.

This ethos is precisely why WordPress powers over 35% of all sites on the internet. It's not just about code but a global community–it is a common language among bloggers, publishers, hobbyists, developers, and big enterprise companies. Together we're building the operating system for the open web.

From hosting and plugins to ecommerce, Peter MacIntyre has written a definitive guide to building with WordPress. Whether you're a career developer or just learning to code, WordPress has something for everyone. Millions of people have turned it into a career, helping millions more build their homes on the open web.

The tools you learn about in this book will serve you well. And if you see something missing, we invite you to build some new roads and make WordPress your own.

Happy building,

– Matt Mullenweg Co-founder, WordPress CEO, Automattic

Dedication

This book is dedicated to the WordPress and PHP communities. These people are amazing, friendly, and giving. You know what "community" truly means, and you live it every day. I have personally met hundreds of people that strive each day to make these products and, therefore, the world a better place. Keep on doing what you do best!

– Peter MacIntyre

I dedicate this book to the PHP Community. It's been a pleasure to be part of it. This community rocks!

– Sávio Resende

Acknowledgments

I want to thank my wife, Dawn, once again for encouraging me daily to be a better person in all areas of life - you are indeed my strong foundation! Of course, thanks also to php[architect] for publishing this book in its second rendition; Oscar continued to see the potential here and made it possible. For the editors and graphics folks who make my scratchings coherent, and for Mr. Mullenweg for his great introduction. Lastly, to my co-author Savio, thanks for your skill, interest, new perspectives, insights, and eagerness to join me on this project. We met at a WordCamp…

Strive for Peace!

– *Peter MacIntyre*

I thank my wife for helping me to be better every day. I'm also thankful to Peter and Oscar for giving me this opportunity to contribute to this book.

– *Sávio Resende*

Biographies

Peter MacIntyre has over 30 years of experience in IT, primarily in the area of PHP and Web Technologies. He has contributed writing material for many industry publications: "Programming PHP", 4th Edition (O'Reilly); "PHP: The Good Parts" (O'Reilly); and "Pro PHP Programming" (APress)—among others.

Peter is a co-founder and past co-chair for the Northeast PHP Developer's Conference previously held in Boston, MA, USA and Charlottetown, PE, Canada (northeastphp.org). As well, Peter has spoken at conferences around the world including "PHP Day" in Verona, Italy; "PHPCE" in Warsaw, Poland; "PHP[World]" in Washington DC, USA; "ZendCon" in Las Vegas, USA; "Prairie Dev Con" in Winnipeg, Canada; "CA-World" in New Orleans, USA; "CA-TechniCon" in Cologne, Germany; and "CA-Expo" in Melbourne, Australia.

He is a Zend Certified Engineer in PHP 5.3 & 4.0 and nomadphp.com PHP Level 1 certified. You can contact him via paladin-bs.com or @pbmacintyre

Sávio Resende has been working with Software Engineering for more than 15 years. He's worked for many companies in the public and private sectors, having had the opportunity to build and maintain the Construction Management System for the Education Ministry and the Publishing System for the Health Ministry, both for Brazil's Federal Government. Between the private sector's projects, he worked in projects that served MIT, London's Metropolitan Archives, Primero Imports, STM Group, and Costco Hearing Aid Centre.

Sávio is a Co-Organizer of the Ottawa PHP Meetup and helps promote the technology to new heights. He also participated on the Vancouver PHP Meetup while he lived there. Sávio is originally from Brazil and now lives in Ottawa, Canada, with his wife Marina and a yellow labrador called Snoopy.

Chapter

1

Planning a Website

These days, the needs of a website is a daunting topic. When approaching your needs, you have to be very specific in what you want your site to do and who your intended audience is. This chapter discusses websites in a broader sense to help you think along these lines. We hope to help you answer some of the following questions.

Overview

Design and architecture questions to consider. Here is a brief list of items to help you find what you want your web presence to be and do. In the following sections, we will explore how WordPress answers most of these questions. Depending on the theme and your selected plugins, you can answer all of these questions, but keep in mind that "how" you want these questions answered is just as important. The answers to these questions may determine what plugins and themes you employ on your site.

1. What do I want my website to do?
2. What will my website look like?
3. How do I protect my content?
4. Who will be accessing my site as an administrator?
5. Do I want to sell anything on my site?

Give some thought to who will be using your site. A successful website is one that users find valuable. Value can come from giving them the right information when they're searching, or selling a product they are shopping for.

6. Who will be my audience?
7. Where will my audience be located?
8. Do most of my users use a desktop or laptop PC, tablets, or mobile phones?
9. How will I reach my audience?
10. How will my audience find me?
11. How do I communicate with my audience?

You should also have a plan for keeping your site up to date and useful once it's launched. Your site needs to adapt and grow as you better understand your audience and change as their needs change.

12. How do I keep my site up to date with content?
13. Do I leverage social media for my site?
14. How do I know if I am accomplishing my goals for my site?

When you're thinking of features your site will provide, it is better to focus on what business problems you need to solve rather than in prescribing exactly how to address them. You may find a plugin that provides a different workflow or user interface you can use to accomplish your goals instead of getting stuck in the depths of attempting to code and implement your own custom prescribed solution. Be sure to look around at different plugins that might partially describe solving your use requirement; with a little thinking and alternative use, it may fit your needs.

Why WordPress?

How does someone facing these concerns and technical issues create a website? What platforms should they consider; what are the options? If you're asking these questions, this is the right book for you! WordPress has 95% of the solutions available natively or via a custom theme and some plugins, and you can achieve the remaining 5% with custom plugin development. This book covers 100% of these aspects. The following sections cover these concerns in broad strokes. The individual chapters that follow offer a deeper dive into each topic. By the end of this book, you will see WordPress is the answer you have been looking for.

Technical Concerns

Responsiveness

How your site renders and works across devices is the most crucial question you need to address. If a large portion of your audience can't see or use your web site, you're bound to fail. Responsiveness means your website is aware of what type of device your visitors are using and automatically adjusts its presentation display. iPhone (vertical), iPhone (horizontal), iPad (vertical), iPad (horizontal), Samsung Galaxy phones, Blackberry phones, desktop monitors—these are just a few of the many devices available to the public. Visitors to your site are likely to use at least two devices (if not more) to interact with your site.

Not long ago, we designed websites for the desktop with mobile devices left as an afterthought, if we considered it at all. More recently, websites are—or should be—designed for mobile devices first and desktop viewing second. When evaluating themes to use on a site, make sure any WordPress theme under consideration implements a responsive design. The theme's description should clearly mention responsiveness. If you are creating a custom theme, let your designer know you expect it to be responsive across all major/popular devices. While this does not guarantee your site will look fantastic on all devices without any work, it does give you a responsive foundation to build upon. Full responsiveness is then controlled with custom coded CSS (Cascading Style Sheets). See Chapter 3 for guidance on this subject. A desktop view of your site usually looks fairly different than the mobile version due to screen real estate and desired functionality. Be sure you and your web developer understand how this relates to the responsiveness of your site. This discussion should answer most of question number two in our list above.

1. Planning a Website

Figure 1.1. WordPress.org in a desktop browser

Figure 1.2. Mobile view of WordPress.org

Default Themes

WordPress comes with a few default themes that are updated often and have some useful features. WordPress names its themes after the year that they are released. So you may see themes called "Twenty Nineteen" and "Twenty Twenty." These themes are great for getting started or if you want a basic site that doesn't need a lot of additional features. The newest ones are responsive and you can use them to quickly prototype how your content might look.

Keeping Content Current

This is the ongoing concern of blogs and other sites built to have returning visitors. Do you hire a content creator? Who is editing your content for typos, grammatical mistakes, and polish? How often is adding new content adequate to maintain readers' interests? Once a week, once a month, every day? If you plan to create a site with these needs, you must address some of these questions.

WordPress has this covered on a few fronts. If you have a lot of content readily available, you should consider the scheduling aspect of this platform. You can prepare multiple posts in WordPress and schedule when they should be published. You can schedule the releases one week apart or at your convenience, and your content will remain "fresh" even though you had it prepared ahead of time. By doing so, you can block off time to write posts and let WordPress release them throughout the week or month.

Another thing WordPress can do with the aid of a plugin is to allow your readers to sign up for email notifications of when posts go live. Doing so allows for the site visitor to receive notification of additions or changes to your site. Return visitors are valuable since they've already expressed an interest in your site.

Should you have a team of content creators, there are other considerations, such as administrative access. WordPress allows for different levels of site access without having total administrator access. Be sure not to give out administrator access to everyone. Instead, try to give each user only as much access as they need to do their tasks. Someone who posts new content shouldn't be able to change your theme or install plugins. The WordPress Codex has a page describing the "Default Roles and Capabilities"[1] available. With this technique, you can have others add content to your site without having the power to totally mess it up!

---

[1] "Default Roles and Capabilities": https://wordpress.org/support/article/roles-and-capabilities/

Ecommerce

If you are planning to make a web store to sell something, even if it's a virtual product like access to webinar videos, you need to connect to an ecommerce package. This package would then, in turn, tie into a financial platform like PayPal[2] or Stripe[3] for processing payments from your customer. You'll need to register for an account with one of them before you can accept credit card payments.

There is some planning needed when considering how to roll this out. You should carefully plan how to handle pricing, discounts, shipping, quantity, financial platform, credit card, refunds, and so on before going live. The number one plugin for this on WordPress is WooCommerce. It has many add-on plugins that can make your site more easily managed and efficient.

Multilingual

Your answer to question number three dictates whether you need a multi-language website. We cover multi-language issues in Chapter 7 concerning plugin and theme development. If you decide you want to have a completely multi-language website, be sure to check out the "xili-language" plugin[4]. When developing a fully multi-lingual site, keep in mind there are many issues to address, such as menu wording, page naming, what languages you will use, duplicating content, SEO for each language, and so on.

Operational Considerations

Search Engine Optimization (SEO)

SEO attempts to structure the content on a page, including headings, the URL, and metadata, such as descriptions, keywords, and page titles. It helps search engines like Google and Bing find pages on your site and include them in their search index. Other factors, like page load speed and mobile-friendly designs, are also considered when generating search result pages. The ultimate goal is for your site to place prominently on the list of returned search items when someone does a search matching content on your site. This helps, in part, to answer questions nine and ten above.

Search Engine Optimization is a well-honed skill unto itself. Companies specialize in this one aspect of web design alone. What you do with SEO answers questions five and six above. Chapter 9 has a section on Yoast's SEO plugin; be sure to study that section as you plan for ways to get discovered.

---

[2]   PayPal: https://paypal.com
[3]   Stripe: https://stripe.com
[4]   "xili-language" plugin: https://wordpress.org/plugins/xili-language

Reaching Your Users

Besides using SEO techniques to help others find your site, you can employ more proactive techniques. You can start an email list for site visitors to sign up to receive email notifications. Better yet, you can have them "like" your content on social media and thus bring attention to you through those platforms. There is a plugin called Shareaholic[5], which allows site visitors to like and share your site's posts and pages. Vistors can raise awareness for your site on social media. Organic leads and recommendations of this sort are invaluable.

User Analytics

One of the most valuable aspects of hosting a website is seeing who has reached your site, from where they accessed it, and how often they did so. Some of the most useful statistics that can be gathered are items like unique page views, unique site visitors, visitor location, bounce rate, page load time, and more. These can be filtered down over 30 days, 14 days, seven days, yesterday, and custom ranges. The site owner can see whether a particular sale, social media campaign, or specific post is drawing any attention and may allow for a change or pivot in tactics. These stats may also help you sell advertising space on your popular site to other marketers. You can prove your site has high or desirable traffic and, therefore, available "eyes" for their advertising. At the very least, it shows the popularity of your site over time.

Enter Google Analytics. This free Google tool is invaluable for guiding your marketing and sales thrusts for your site if marketing and sales are essential to you. The statistics Google Analytics provides, help you fine-tune your efforts, and adjust your SEO if needed. Chapter 9 has a section on the plugin called Google Analytics Dashboard for WP. So be sure to look into this plugin. Attention to Google Analytics' information helps you answer question number eleven from our list above.

Keep in mind these statistics can be blocked by some browser add-on tools or firewall settings. Some people don't like Google tracking them at all, even though they are usually aggregated into a summary number. Still, it behooves us as web developers to be sensitive to these concerns and handle the gathered numerical information with care. An alternative to Google is the free, open-source tool called Matomo[6], so check that out if you share some of these concerns.

---

[5] Shareaholic: https://www.shareaholic.com
[6] Matomo: https://matomo.org

Also, as a partial answer to question seven, be sure to review the requirements for GDPR[7] as it relates to EU (European Union) citizens (and their personal data) who may visit your website.

Security

Question number nine is vital, no matter the purpose of our site. Keeping WordPress as secure as possible is extremely important. You don't want your site hacked. You don't want your content to suddenly be contrary to your image or what you want to portray to the online world. In WordPress, there are two types of vulnerabilities.

The first part of site protection is more general in coverage. You can be attacked in many ways, some as simple as a malicious user correctly guessing your administrator password. Make sure you pick a unique and long password for your admin accounts. Don't use this password on other websites.

WordFence is an excellent free security plugin and is discussed in Chapter 9. iThemes Security[8]—a commercial option—and Jetpack Security[9]—part of the Jetpack multi-plugin—are two other plugins to consider for site security if you need to be extra secure! These plugins keep a running list of site vulnerabilities and watch for site attacks by humans or bots. They can alert you by email and block the IP addresses of attempts to guess your passwords, exploit known insecure plugins, etc.

Another aspect of site security is the administration access typically accessed by adding /wp-admin to the website's URL. Since this is a standard for WordPress, it can be an access point for security breaches and is frequently targeted by automated attacks. Consider using the plugin called "Protect Your Admin."[10] to customize your admin login URL to a location you name yourself. Make sure you pick something unique and not easily guessed. This practice makes sure only those who know the redirected URL can access the admin area.

---

[7]   GDPR: https://eugdpr.org
[8]   iThemes Security: https://ithemes.com/security
[9]   Jetpack Security: https://jetpack.com/features/security
[10] "Protect Your Admin.": https://wordpress.org/plugins/protect-wp-admin/

Figure 1.3.

Comment Spam

Another issue you can face are unwanted comments to your posts—comment spam. It may not be a "real" security risk, but it's damn annoying. To control this, you can either turn off comments site-wide or force comments to be approved by the site administrators. See Settings > Discussion for options on this (Figure 1.3).

If you do want to allow comments and site feedback but want to filter it, you can use the Akismet plugin to help with filtering spam submissions. Chapter 8 has a section covering this plugin.

Chapter

2

Development Environment Requirements

HTML and CSS

This book assumes you have a basic understanding of both HTML and CSS (Cascading Style Sheets) mark up. If you are not well-versed in these technologies, then please use your favorite search engine for assistance. We do have a crash course in chapter three, but for more in-depth coverage, be sure to seek answers on the web. W3Schools[1] is a great place to start, and, of course, there are many books out there to consider picking up and going through.

---

[1] W3Schools: http://www.w3schools.com

Overview

Apache Web Server

Apache[2] is a popular web server. Most web hosting companies use this as their defacto web server, although others like IIS from Microsoft and NGINX are available. Apache, or another web server of your choice, is the platform from which you serve your web content and handles responding to requests from browsers and other HTTP clients. In some setups, your web server—and possibly the database server—runs in a virtual environment or a container like Docker, Vagrant, or Calico.

PHP

PHP[3] is the web development language running almost 80% of the web. It is the main programming language used by WordPress as well. PHP started as a scripting language in June 1995 and has not grown since, adding features version after version. The latest version, 7.4 at the time of this writing, provides a speed increase version with a few new features. When you are looking for a hosting company, be sure they at least support PHP version 7.2 In general, look for a hosting company that uses a version still supported by the PHP core team. The core team maintains a list of the supported versions[4] online.

At the time of writing, WordPress.org recommends[5] using PHP 7.3 at a minimum, although WordPress can run in older versions.

MySQL or MariaDB

MySQL is the database platform that usually ties in with PHP. They work very well together, but MySQL is not the only database PHP can connect to. For a full list, see the supported database vendors[6]. MariaDB is a variant—or "fork" —of MySQL, more firmly placed in the open-source arena that attempts to keep compatibility with the core of the MySQL product. The developers forked it from the main MySQL codebase, citing concerns that the current owners of MySQL (ORACLE Corp.) might not do their best to keep it as a fully open-source product.

Keep in mind, WordPress only works on MySQL or MariaDB. When we get into the chapters on plugin development and child themes, we will be looking at PHP code, Word-Press functions written in PHP, and database connections to MySQL. You should be at least familiar with these technologies if you plan to do any WordPress development.

---

[2]   Apache: https://httpd.apache.org
[3]   PHP: https://php.net
[4]   supported versions: https://www.php.net/supported-versions.php
[5]   recommends: https://phpa.me/wordpress-requirements
[6]   database vendors: https://php.net/refs.database.vendors

Development Platforms

Before we get into the nitty-gritty of WordPress, let's discuss the broader topic of development environments versus production environments and how to install these products in each. There are a few schools of thought on how many environments are needed, from development to research and development to staging to production.

The development environment is where you add new features to your project and try them out. It is an environment where you can experiment with ideas with few inhibitions on what you may want to try out. Every developer working on an application should have their own development environment. This site should use placeholder content for testing that does not use sensitive information like real customer accounts. Doing so prevents you from leaking it accidentally or mangling it via an error in plugin code.

The staging platform is the place to push your new ideas to a select group of reviewers and testers to prove your ideas and concepts. Use it to confirm changes made in your experimental environment work as intended and can be accepted by stakeholders before you release it to the entire world.

Production is the platform serving your live, publicly accessible site. It may be a single server or one shared with others. For larger sites, it may be composed of multiple web servers, database servers, and other services like load balancers and caches.

At the very least, you should have a development platform separate from your live production environment. You certainly don't want to attempt to use a new plugin and go through setting up on your live site only to find it doesn't work as expected. You don't want to risk any data loss or unplanned downtime in production caused by a misconfigured plugin or a bug in code. Given the bare minimum of development and production platforms, this begs the question of where you should host these environments.

Minimize "It Works on My Machine"

You may think this should go without saying. Still, it must be said—try your absolute best to have the platforms, primarily their underlying technologies: PHP, MySQL, Web server, and WordPress, of both environments configured identically. You may not have this ideal development environment of multiple identical platforms available to you, or you may want to develop in your favorite operating system and deploy to a different operating system platform for production. You may want to develop on your local desktop environment for speed and convenience rather than depend on the host production environment. But keep in mind that the more different these environments are from each other, the chances of grief arising, as a result, are higher. With virtualization and container tools available, you can have nearly identical development and production setups with minimal effort.

Server Platforms Environments

As you can see, the options are many and varied. Here are some helpful links to guide you in setting up a hosting platform regardless of the physical location. Each of these aims to provide a means to easily install all the software components needed to run and serve a WordPress environment. You would, however, still need to install WordPress on top of these environments.

The following are good options for you if you set up a development environment on your personal computer. There is no need to do this if you are using a hosting platform like Bluehost, HostGator, or GoDaddy as this should be all set up and maintained for you. In this case, you'll still need to set up a development domain separate from your production one.

MAMP

MAMP stands for Apple's **M**ac (operating system), **A**pache (web server software), **M**ySQL (database software), and **P**HP (Web development language). It allows you to serve an environment locally on any Mac (iOS) computer. Use their download page[7] to get started with the software bundled for you.

MAMP also provides extensive documentation[8] for installation and set up.

LAMP

LAMP stands for **L**inux operating system, **A**pache, **M**ySQL, and **P**HP. Your exact flavor of Linux may vary and is based on a distribution like Ubuntu, Debian, Red Hat, CentOS, or more. This platform can quickly be installed on an existing local Linux system and used for development platform work. Follow one of these guides to installing LAMP[9] for various Linux environments.

WAMP

WAMP[10] stands for Windows (operating system), Apache, MySQL, and PHP. This platform can easily be installed on your local Windows system and used for development platform work.

---

[7]   download page: *https://www.mamp.info/en/downloads*
[8]   documentation: *https://documentation.mamp.info*
[9]   installing LAMP: *https://phpa.me/linode-lamp-guides*
[10] WAMP: *http://www.wampserver.com/en*

Flywheel

Flywheel[11] is specially designed for creating local WordPress development environments. It can be installed on both Mac and Windows platforms and has all the underlying technologies incorporated into it. One key feature of this tool is that you can develop WordPress sites locally and share them with project stakeholders from your local environment. This feature reduces the need for a separate staging environment.

Other Platforms

For a more general discussion on development stacks, refer to "WordPress Installation Techniques"[12] and these instructions for setting up a development environment[13].

As a final note to this environment discussion, you can use subdomains to perform development before setting up a production site. For example, if the WordPress site's production destination is going to be `river-thames.com` then on a development server, we can create the subdomain: `riverthames.example.com` or perhaps `dev.river-thames.com`. The subdomains you end up using may depend on the access you have to configure DNS, particularly for clients.

Having both environments on the same web hosting platform like Bluehost or GoDaddy is ideal. This also lends itself well to moving content from development to production (deployment) as folders, file names, and file locations would all be similar if not identical. Doing so also minimizes subtle bugs that can arise if the underlying platform uses different versions of the web server, MySQL server, or PHP interpreter.

WordPress Install

WordPress extolls their five-minute installation process[14], but there is a little more to setting up WordPress. Getting the right configuration and default plugins is also helpful to have ready to go. So unless you are in a mad rush to get WordPress up and running, you should consider the following more calculated approach.

After you have set up your hosting environment and have an administration account for securely connecting to the platform's FTP access and have downloaded the install files for WordPress, you are ready to set up the default WordPress environment. By this, we mean having all the files and plugins you regularly use ready to be uploaded. See Figure 2.1 for the listing of a standard WordPress file structure.

---

[11] Flywheel: https://localbyflywheel.com
[12] "WordPress Installation Techniques": https://phpa.me/wp-install-techniques
[13] development environment: https://phpa.me/wp-setup-dev
[14] five-minute installation process: https://phpa.me/codex-5-minute

Here you see the folder called WordPress_511 (1) where a basic install is kept. After finishing a basic installation and removing useless default plugins like "Hello Dolly", we installed two plugins we employ on every environment (development to production), namely Akismet and WordFence (2). See chapters eight and nine for details on these two plugins. Then we reconnect (via secure FTP) to the host and upload the entire WordPress file structure. From here on, we have the default installation that we want with our desired preloaded plugins already installed. We can then upload this file structure as often as we need to each subsequent WordPress project. See the section below for alternate methods of deployment and updating of WordPress.

Figure 2.1.

> *Some hosting companies have started to include basic WordPress installations as a feature of their hosting environments. While this is a faster way to get things going from a basic WordPress installation point of view, you have to make sure you have the plugins you wanted and the basic settings for the overall environment. In the long run, it may be more straightforward and time-efficient to make your basic install, as discussed in the previous section, especially if you are a web developer that creates many sites for multiple clients in the run of a month.*

wp-config Settings

After you have uploaded your new default files, the next thing you want to do is edit the WordPress configuration file (wp-config.php) to allow WordPress to connect to the database you are using on your host for each particular installation. The database name and admin accesses are set up ahead of time on the hosting platform. If you can, edit this file after you upload it to the server. If you can't edit it on the server, make the changes locally and upload it after you save your changes. Regardless, make the changes shown in Listing 2.1 to wp-config.php.

Listing 2.1

```
 1. // ** MySQL settings - You can get this info from your web host ** //
 2. /** The name of the database for WordPress */
 3. define( 'DB_NAME', 'database_name_here' ); // (1)
 4.
 5. /** MySQL database username */
 6. define( 'DB_USER', 'username_here' ); // (2)
 7.
 8. /** MySQL database password */
 9. define( 'DB_PASSWORD', 'password_here' ); // (3)
10.
11.
12. /** Increase Memory for WordPress */
13. define ( 'WP_MEMORY_LIMIT', '96M' ); // (4)
14.
15. /** Increase Execution time for WordPress **/
16. set_time_limit(60); // (5)
17.
18. define( 'FTP_HOST', 'ftp.example.com' ); //(5)
19. define( 'FTP_USER', 'FTPUSER' );
20. define( 'FTP_PASS', 'FTPPASS' );
```

1. Provide the name of the database that you are using on this host.
2. Provide the name of the database user account that has access to the named database on this host.
3. Provide the password of the database user account that has access to the named database on this host.
4. If you want to attempt to increase the memory usage of the default installation of PHP on your server (if you are using a commercial host like Bluehost or GoDaddy), define the setting of WP_MEMORY_LIMIT and set it to 96M. This allows your site to better handle page loading and, therefore, serve your site visitors on a more stable footing (not crashing by running out of memory). This setting often defaults to 8 or 16 megabytes by hosting providers. Be aware that some hosts curtail the editing of this option, and you won't be allowed to alter this value, but it's always worth it to attempt to change this value for your site's stability.
5. If you don't want to be asked every time you add or update a plugin on your site, make the changes for FTP access in this configuration file.

Save your changes and then open a browser to run the WordPress set up routines of your new site. WordPress recognizes that when you first visit your site, it has not been installed and tries to run its configuration routines. With our previous example on the development environment, you would type in the following URL: http://riverthames.example.com. You should see something like what is shown in Figure 2.2, offering you the language selection as the first step in the setup process.

Autoupdate (Yea or Nay?)

As of WordPress version 3.7, an automatic update process was added to the core of the product. Malicious actors target older versions of software with known vulnerabilities. An effective way to deter them is to keep your software up-to-date.

Figure 2.2.

Any updates for maintenance or security reasons are automatically performed when the WordPress Development team releases them. Other significant updates like full version updates—from version 4 to 5, for example—are still under the user's control and discretion. You can override this feature if you want to, but for your self-preservation, you should seriously consider the ramifications if you do disable this process. Plugins are left for you to update manually except where they may affect the overall security of a WordPress site. See the discussion on WordFence in Chapter 9 for help on being notified when updates are pending.

If you want to override this functionality, add a directive to the `wp-config.php` file with the following line:

```
define('AUTOMATIC_UPDATER_DISABLED', true);
```

This constant completely disables all updates on the entire site. If you want to be more precise in what you allow for updates, you can use the following directive:

```
define('WP_AUTO_UPDATE_CORE', false);
```

The second option has three possible values: `true`, `false`, and `minor`. `true` enables development updates—you would have to be using a development (unreleased) version of WordPress for this to affect developmental features. On other sites, this means that only major and minor core updates are automatically updated. If set to `false`, WordPress does not automatically install any development updates. `minor` means only minor updates are updated and that both developmental and major core updates are disabled.

For a full discussion on this topic and all its nuances, read "Configuring Automatic Background Updates"[15].

Deploying and Updating WordPress

There are more modern ways to deploy (install) your WordPress than the manual process that we have discussed above. For example, you can deploy using Git[16], a tool for managing versions of source code. You can set up a GitHub repository with a minimal installation of WordPress. Then via webhooks, you can trigger updates to as many other installations of WordPress as you want. This process works well if you have many sites you want to keep up-to-date and only want to do the update process once, having the effects ripple through all your related sites. The webhook can be triggered every time a "push" update occurs on the master repository. For details on this approach, consider this article on "WordPress Deployment Part 3: Deploying WordPress Using Git"[17].

Another method of updating is similar to the initial installation approach mentioned in the section above. Using (S)FTP to connect to your installation and upload any new files you desire. The drawback here is that you could potentially miss a file or replace the wrong folder, and nothing gets done, or you mess up the entire WordPress installation with a difficult "road back." Be careful using this method beyond the initial setup of the overall WordPress site. When FTP is the only way to connect to a site, an FTP client like lftp[18] can automatically synchronize two directories, saving time and preventing errors.

The last approach, which is the most stable, is to use the WordPress Administration area to update plugins and core WordPress files. Using this approach, you can control exactly what plugins or themes you want to update on each specific WordPress installation that you want. This method is the most straightforward—although the most labor-intensive—if you have multiple sites to update. For that scenario, products are available on the web to manage multiple WordPress sites and their updates all at once. The drawback here is that they are not free and may not have the finite control you are looking for—updating one plugin on one site and not on another for some specific reason. A few of these multi-site control platforms are ManageWP[19], WP Remote[20], and iControlWP[21].

---

[15] *"Configuring Automatic Background Updates": https://phpa.me/wp-config-auto-update*
[16] *Git: https://git-scm.com*
[17] *"WordPress Deployment Part 3: Deploying WordPress Using Git": https://phpa.me/wp-deployment-git*
[18] *lftp: https://lftp.yar.ru/features.html*
[19] *ManageWP: https://managewp.com*
[20] *WP Remote: https://wpremote.com*
[21] *iControlWP: https://www.icontrolwp.com*

Backing Up a WordPress Site

You should always backup your WordPress installations once they are holding more than your initial installation data. If your site gets compromised or a rogue plugin deletes your data, you can minimize data losses. You don't want to lose any information and have it gone forever. That would be a disaster!

Use the plugin covered in chapter nine called "All-in-One Migration", which doubles as a complete WordPress site backup tool, including the underlying database. Be sure to get this in operation or something similar before doing any major site updates.

Chapter

3

CSS Crash Course

This chapter is for people who want to understand the main elements of CSS and learn how to use it. While it covers the basics, we strongly recommend having a previous understanding of HTML. For further reference, visit the core W3C references to get started with HTML[1] and CSS[2].

---

[1]   HTML: *https://dev.w3.org/html5/*
[2]   CSS: *https://www.w3schools.com/css/*

HTML

To begin with CSS, we first have to understand what HTML is and how it works. Known as a markup language, HTML is the language browsers interpret when rendering webpages. HTML stands for Hypertext Markup Language, and it has been around since 1991.

HTML provides the structure of what we call HTML Documents, also known as webpages. We'll see an example shortly. As we'll see, HTML can be extended and manipulated via JavaScript or CSS. If we fragment HTML into smaller pieces to see what it is built with, we find nodes. To avoid getting too deep in the technical specification of HTML, and to keep it short, you should know HTML inherits the XML[3] *Nodes Tree* model. This *Nodes Tree* in HTML is known as a DOM Tree. DOM stands for Document Object Model, and we use it:

> *"(…) to represent the structure and state of the elements in the document being rendered by a user agent."*
>
> From HTML to Platform Accessibility APIs Implementation Guide[4], 2020

A *user agent* is usually a browser, like Firefox, Chrome, or Safari. However, it can also be other clients like a search engine's spider that know how to make HTTP requests. The DOM is a data structure that keeps the document's information. The information that the DOM keeps is the **state** and the **structure** of the webpage. They are implemented with **nodes** and **attributes** added to them.

What is a node? Well, a node is an element that looks like this:

```
<p id="paragraph-one">some content</p>
```

The preceding example is a node that, in HTML, this is best known as "p tag." This tag's purpose is to indicate a paragraph. Each HTML tag has a purpose, and some tags' purposes are more adaptable than others. To utilize this flexibility and select the correct tags to use, you need to know how many "inherited properties" the element comes with by default, which attributes are required, and what optional attributes it supports. Some tags do not afford much customization.

These attributes can specify either behavior or style. One example of behavior customization we have is tables as in Listing 3.1.

---

[3] XML: *https://www.w3.org/XML/Datamodel.html*
[4] HTML to Platform Accessibility APIs Implementation Guide: *https://phpa.me/html-api-map*

Listing 3.1

```
1. <table>
2.     <tr>
3.         <td colspan="2">Column 1 and 2</td>
4.     </tr>
5.     <tr>
6.         <td>Column 1</td>
7.         <td>Column 2</td>
8.     </tr>
9. </table>
```

The colspan attribute specifies that the <td> cell in the first row, <tr>, spans across two table columns. Note how we don't have to specify how many rows or columns the <table> contains first—the browser figures that out based on the row and cell tags we include.

An example of a style specification is as follows:

```
<p style="color: blue;">Some blue test</p>
```

This attribute tells the browser to render the text inside the <p> tag blue.

In these examples, we customize the state and structure of the DOM via attributes. Even though this is the built-in way of customizing HTML elements, the most common way to extend and manipulate it is via JavaScript and CSS. You might ask: If attributes specify state or structure, what is the id doing in the first paragraph example? It identifies the element by a unique identifier that we cover later.

Every attribute in HTML determines a specific aspect of a node, and each id is responsible for unique identifications of nodes. When we give an element an id, that element can be found by a unique identifier either in CSS styles or through JavaScript. Each id attribute in an HTML document must be unique, and the user experience is affected by that. Visiting a URL like: https://www.phparch.com/#body, should open the page scrolled directly at the point in the HTML document where the element marked with the attribute id="body" is visible. It's helpful when you want to bookmark a specific point in the document, typically a heading, and give users a link to go directly to that point in the text.

> *Semantically, you can certainly give an element an ID of* body *for users to scroll to automatically. However, don't confuse it with the* <body> *tag that follows the* <head> *tag.*

3. CSS CRASH COURSE

The basic structure of an HTML document looks like Listing 3.2.

Listing 3.2

```
1. <!DOCTYPE html>
2. <html>
3. <head>
4.     <meta charset="UTF-8">
5.     <title>Title of the document</title>
6. </head>
7.
8. <body>
9. Content of the document......
10. </body>
11.
12. </html>
```

Browsers render the tags found between the opening and closing <body> tags. The <header> is the part with the metadata about your document. Search engines and user agents (e.g., browsers) use it to discover details like the language of your page, the title to present in the browser's tab, CSS and JavaScript files to load alongside the document, keywords, and descriptions for search engines.

HTML has seen several iterations since its creation. With every new version, the community has enhanced its functionality to make it more useful and meet new requirements. The current version is HTML5, which has innovations like new HTML elements, deprecated elements, and new APIs. While we won't go into these features here, you can see the official reference of the current standard here[5]. If you need a quick list of those changes, this HTML 5 intro[6] is a useful reference.

An HTML file is saved as a plain-text; all you need to work with them is a basic text editor. Don't use a word processor like Microsoft Word or Pages, which saves documents in a proprietary format. They add many invisible elements, some similar to XML, and you won't be able to build proper HTML pages with such applications.

---

[5] here: https://html.spec.whatwg.org/multipage/
[6] HTML 5 intro: https://www.w3schools.com/html/html5_intro.asp

Style Sheets

What are **Cascading Style Sheets**? They are descriptive statements of how HTML elements should be displayed. A few examples of the characteristics you can customize with CSS include text colors, text underline, font size, text justification, block visibility, and block opacity.

In the process of building a webpage, CSS defines how HTML elements are presented related to others. We specify all of this through **CSS Rules**.

To understand CSS better, it is essential to understand its origins. When HTML was new, writers of webpages didn't have sufficient control over how their pages looked. Designers were limited to tweaking a few things like fonts and colors. Most design elements were introduced via adding images. CSS grew out of this need, and later HTML evolved beyond static documents and into web applications. CSS gained popularity after the conference "Mosaic and the Web," where:

> *"Dave Raggett, a main architect of HTML 3.0, realized that HTML would and should never turn into a page-description language and that a more purpose-built mechanism was needed to satisfy requirements from authors."*
>
> *– From "A brief history of CSS until 2016"*[7]

CSS wasn't the only style language proposed, but it gained acceptance by being "cascaded" and straightforward. The cascading attribute is crucial; it's still a defining factor today. The webpage presentation is a combination of the author's wishes and device/browser capabilities. Keep in mind, your application doesn't look the same across devices. We're also limited by the browser, the customizations available depending on the technology generation, and other factors. Especially for new features, it's vital to check the documentation for rules that you decide to use when building your web pages to ensure they are adequately supported. CSS Rules are added or deprecated in every version of CSS.

CSS rules are composed of **selectors** and **declarations**. We cover the selectors first, and how to accomplish responsiveness with declarations. For you to understand further the options for declarations, we provide some useful references.

---

[7] "A brief history of CSS until 2016": https://www.w3.org/Style/CSS20/history.html

About CSS Versions

The current version of CSS is 3, and is known as "CSS Level 3". This name is to differentiate the current way of building the CSS Standard from the previous methods. The old way is known as "monolithic," which indicates an enormous source code base having everything. It makes it more challenging to incorporate new requirements as they come. The CSS Level 3 builds upon CSS Level 2 by grouping new features in modules, making it easier for specific modules to evolve independently. Some might have demands to adapt faster than others. The module approach makes it possible to iterate more quickly, allowing one feature to have a "level 4" before other features get to "level 2."

Syntax

CSS syntax consists of selectors and declarations. The selector points to one or more HTML elements a group of declarations affects. The declaration is surrounded by curly brackets { } and has two parts—the properties and their values. The following basic example shows how to style the h1 HTML tag used for first-level headings on a page.

```
h1 {
    font-size: 16px;
    text-decoration: underline;
}
```

This declaration relates to an HTML element through a selector. However, it is also possible to add the CSS declaration directly into the HTML element with the style attribute. This is known as an inline declaration:

```
<h1 style="font-size: 16px;text-decoration: underline;">
    My Title
</h1>
```

Inline styles are ideal when keeping components modular, and you can reuse them without too much difficulty. Manually updating all the inline styles affecting all your h1 tags gets tedious quickly. Using inline styles is heavily debated by web designers, and the conclusion changes according to the context. It makes code harder to maintain and more rigid, but modern JavaScript view libraries such as ReactJS, frequently use inline declarations automatically.

Common Properties

Now that you have a better idea of how CSS works, let's take a look at some frequently used basic properties. The table below describes the syntax for often customized properties.

Property	Example	Description
Color	p { color: blue; }	Sets a color for the text at an element.
Background Color	div { background-color: gray }	Sets the background color for the referenced div tag.
Margin	div { margin: 10px; }	Sets the margin for an element (external spacing). This is the short-hand of the more specific attributes margin-top, margin-right, margin-bottom and margin-left.
Padding	div { padding: 10px }	Sets the padding for an element (internal spacing).
Height	div { height: 150px }	The height of a block element.
Width	div { width: 450px }	The width of a block element.

Selectors

CSS uses selectors and understanding how selectors work is crucial for learning how CSS works. Consider the example in Listing 3.3.

Listing 3.3

```
1. <!DOCTYPE html>
2. <html>
3. <head>
4.     <meta charset="utf-8">
5.     <title>CSS Crash Course</title>
6.     <link rel="stylesheet" href="style.css">
7. </head>
8. <body>
9. <h1>CSS Crash Course</h1>
10. <p>...serving not simply webpages, but pieces of art.</p>
11. </body>
12. </html>
```

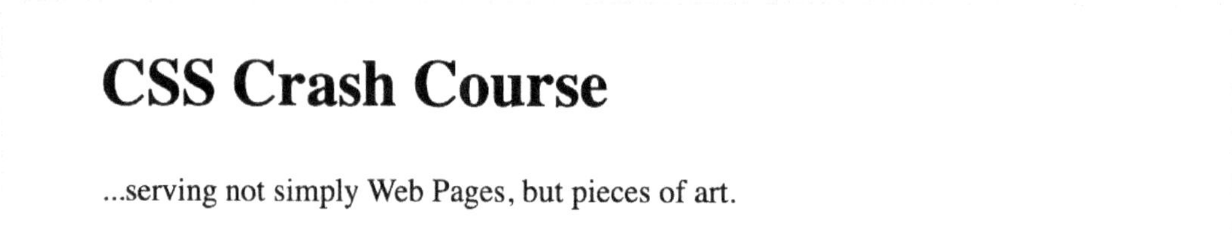

CSS Crash Course

...serving not simply Web Pages, but pieces of art.

Figure 3.1.

Without the CSS, it looks like Figure 3.1.

With the CSS in Listing 3.4, a user's browser renders something similar to Figure 3.2. With two rules, we're able to customize how headings and paragraphs display.

Listing 3.4

```
1.  h1 {
2.      color: #000;
3.      background-color: #cfcfcf;
4.      border: 1px solid black;
5.      border-radius: 6px;
6.      padding: 10px;
7.      font-size: 18px;
8.      text-align: center;
9.  }
10.
11. p {
12.     color: #000;
13.     text-align: right;
14.     margin-right: 30px;
15.     font-style: italic;
16. }
```

CSS Crash Course

...serving not simply Web Pages, but pieces of art.

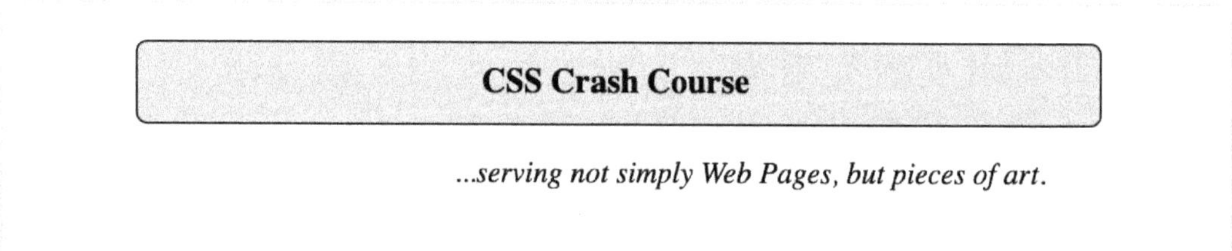

Figure 3.2.

Including CSS Rules

Within an HTML document, you can use style tags or link tags to define CSS rules to use with your document. Style tags typically include the rules right in your document. Link tags tell browsers to load and use a separate file with your styles.

External Style Sheets

As you can see, the HTML file is invoking the CSS by the `<link>` tag at this line:

```
<link rel="stylesheet" href="style.css">
```

It shows one of the possible ways of including a specific CSS into your webpage. Linking to style sheets in this way provides the following benefits:

- You and your designers can version your style sheet with a tool like Git.
- Your style sheet is cached by visitors browsers, which reduces the load on your server and speeds subsequent page renders.
- You can reuse files across pages, to make your look-and-feel consistent and maintainable with less effort.

Versioning and caching work together to speed up page loading. To prevent clients from downloading the same styles, your style sheets are cached based on factors like the file name, last modified time, and server-side cache control headers. Client-side caching speeds up page loading and rendering to improve your visitor's UX. It prevents clients from downloading the same style sheet for every page load. Instead, they download the file once and use the cached copy on all pages. This technique saves your servers from serving that same style sheet on multiple requests and frees up web server resources.

Caching leads to one problem, however. How do you ensure people download the newest version of a file when you deploy updates? Your web server might tell visitors to use a cached file for months or years in the future. A common way to bust caches when you update is to add a version parameter to your style sheet's URL like this in your HTML:

```
<link rel="stylesheet" href="style.css?v=1">
```

Notice the ?v=1. That part specifies the version of your style sheet. To inform the browsers to download the new version when you have a new version, update your HTML code with a new version number like ?v=2. When it comes to reusing CSS, it is useful for building a library of styles that can be reused on new pages and include the style sheet with the `<link>`. You can load as many style sheets as you want. You can create base style sheets to specify a design direction for entire projects. Doing so can save days of work while reducing risks and increasing the consistency of the presentation of your webpages. Popular

3. CSS Crash Course

CSS frameworks, which are examples of CSS reuse, are available including Bootstrap[8] and Materialize[9]. There are many others. By adding Bootstrap CSS to your page, for example, you "inherit" all the styles specified by that framework. Frameworks allow you to follow standards and use fancy effects out-of-the-box with minimal design, instead of building them yourself. After adding it, you only need to add your styles for small customizations where needed.

Style Tags

Another way to include CSS is to use a style tag (`<style></style>`) in the same HTML file. Listing 3.5 is the same example, but implementing style tags.

Listing 3.5

```
1.  <!DOCTYPE html>
2.  <html>
3.  <head>
4.      <meta charset="utf-8">
5.      <title>CSS Crash Course</title>
6.      <style>
7.          h1 {
8.              color: #000;
9.              background-color: #cfcfcf;
10.             border: 1px solid black;
11.             border-radius: 6px;
12.             padding: 10px;
13.             font-size: 18px;
14.             text-align: center;
15.         }
16.
17.         p {
18.             color: #000;
19.             text-align: right;
20.             margin-right: 30px;
21.             font-style: italic;
22.         }
23.     </style>
24. </head>
25. <body>
26. <h1>CSS Crash Course</h1>
27. <p>...serving not simply webpages, but pieces of art.</p>
28. </body>
29. </html>
```

---

[8]   Bootstrap: https://getbootstrap.com
[9]   Materialize: https://materializecss.com

The disadvantage of this technique is that your HTML file can get very large. File size affects how maintainable your code is, and complicates applying some procedures like optimizations and maintenance. If you use the same CSS across pages, you need to implement a server-side mechanism for including them to avoid copy-pasting them to all the required files. For your site users, inline styles can't be cached and reused across pages. It increases how much data visitors have to download with each page request, which can also slow down page rendering.

Inline Styles

A third way to add style to our elements is using inline styles directly on the tags to customize, as shown in Listing 3.6.

Listing 3.6

```
1.  <!DOCTYPE html>
2.  <html>
3.  <head>
4.      <meta charset="utf-8">
5.      <title>CSS Crash Course</title>
6.  </head>
7.  <body>
8.  <h1 style="color: #000;background-color: #cfcfcf;border: 1px solid
    black;border-radius: 6px;padding: 10px;font-size: 18px;text-align: center;">
9.      CSS Crash Course</h1>
10. <p style="color: #000;text-align: right;margin-right: 30px;font-style:
    italic;">...serving not simply Web Pages, but
11.     pieces of art.</p>
12. </body>
13. </html>
```

The same problems that occur with style tags also apply here. It might be complicated to style the HTML further, quickly using the same settings through multiple pages, if it requires duplicated style for each element.

There is an advantage when the HTML Document is short; it keeps the code independent and componentized. An example of this application is JavaScript libraries/frameworks (such as VueJS or ReactJS), which dynamically apply inline CSS to change the presentation of a webpage. I wouldn't suggest this when working with plain HTML documents without any help from those JavaScript frameworks/libraries.

3. CSS Crash Course

Classes

As we saw, selecting tags is one way to customize HTML styles. Recall in the first CSS file example, we selected all <h1> and <p>tags. In that code, every <h1> and <p> tags are affected in the same way. Using more specific selectors, we can select a subset of <p> tags to have a different presentation. Let's take a look at how to do that using classes.

Class attributes are used to specify an HTML tag belongs to one or more classes. Class names are alphanumeric strings plus - (dash) and _ (underscore); they can't have a number as the first character and must be at least two characters long. Multiple classes for one HTML tag are separated by one or more spaces (" "). Using a class, we can refer to an element in our CSS rules with a . (a dot or period).

```
.page-title {
    color: black;
}
```

We can add this class in our previous HTML like this:

```
<h1 class="page-title">CSS Crash Course</h1>
```

Notice the declaration in the CSS code begins with a period . and the class attribute in the HTML does not. CSS syntax expects class names to start with a period. Omitting the period in the CSS file like in the following code sample is interpreted to mean you are affecting a tag that looks like <page-title></page-title>.

```
page-title {}
```

This selector can select more than one element, and one element can have more than one class. For example, if you have multiple HTML elements with the class "place-title", the same style applies to all of them. If you specify various classes in one element, all of the matching CSS rules affect the given element, depending on the order of classes specified. Latter classes (from left to right) get precedence. This behavior is the "cascading" part of style sheets.

Consider an example (Listing 3.7) of selecting multiple elements with the same class names.

Listing 3.7

```
1. <style>
2.     .place-title {
3.         font-size: 28px;
4.     }
5. </style>
6. <h1 class="page-title">First Place Title</h1>
7. ...
8. <h1 class="place-title">Second Place Title</h1>
9. ...
```

Listing 3.8 is an example of multiple classes affecting the same HTML element. Notice the separation by a space character.

Listing 3.8

```
1.  <style>
2.      .place-title {
3.          font-size: 28px;
4.      }
5.
6.      .place-page-title {
7.          color: blue;
8.      }
9.  </style>
10. <h1 class="place-title place-page-title">First Place Title</h1>
```

IDs

The behavior of class attributes is semantically different from the next selector we're covering: id. It matches any HTML element with the same id attribute. There can be only one identifier in the id attribute, and every id on a page should be unique.

The ID selector starts with a hash character #.

```
#element-id {
    color: blue;
}
```

This selector assumes there is one element with the same ID.

```
<div id="element-id">
 The element.
</div>
```

There are many usages of this selector. Some usages improve user experience (UX). We mentioned one of them earlier when talking about HTML structure (as a reference in the page scrolling position).

Another benefit worth mentioning involves building forms. It improves the accessibility of inputs like text boxes and radio buttons, which usually have labels. When you click on the element or their labels, the cursor moves to the referenced input field. The for attribute of a label controls this behavior. When the input is a radio button or checkbox, they are selected or marked as checked, as you can see in Listing 3.9.

Listing 3.9

```
1. <!-- places the text cursor at the input text once clicked at the label -->
2. <label for="input-one">Input 1</label>
3. <input id="input-one" type="text"/>
4.
5. <!-- checks the correspondent element and it works also for "radio" type -->
6. <label for="option-one">Option 1</label>
7. <input id="option-one" type="checkbox"/>
8. <label for="option-two">Option 2</label>
9. <input id="option-two" type="checkbox"/>
```

Advanced Selectors

Class and ID selectors, as we saw, are two ways of targeting HTML elements to apply CSS rules. Advanced selectors allow you to write rules matching more specific conditions, usually based on the position of HTML elements or other attributes. We can apply these item customizations in many different ways, but we're covering only the most important ones.

It's also worth mentioning one more selector, the attribute selector. The attribute selector works as if we were selecting by ID or class.

In the following example, the selector has a tilde before the equal sign because we want to match links that contain the domain "phparch.com":

```
a[href~="phparch.com"] {
    color: blue;
}
```

In the following HTML, the second link would be in blue text.

```
<p>You can find many resources for programming on
<a href="https://wordpress.org">wordpress.org</a>
and <a href="http://phparch.com">phparch.com</p>
```

We can also add custom attributes to mark them our own way:

```
a[my-custom-attribute="highlight"] {
    color: yellow;
}
```

To use this custom attribute, our HTML would look like the following.

```
<p>This is a regular paragraph</p>
<p my-custom-attribute="highlight">This one is quite important for you to read.</p>
```

Table Of Advanced Selectors

You can build complex expressions to style particular HTML elements. The table summarizes some common examples.

Selector	Example	Description
.class	.intro	Selects all elements with class="intro"
.class1.class2	.name1.name2	Selects all elements with both name1 and name2 set within its class attribute
.class1 .class2	.name1 .name2	Selects all elements with name2 that are a descendant of an element with name1
#id	#firstname	Selects the element with id="firstname"
*	*	Selects all elements
element	p	Selects all <p> elements
element,element	div, p	Selects all <div> elements and all <p> elements
element>element	div > p	Selects all <p> elements where the parent is a <div> element
element+element	div + p	Selects all <p> elements that are placed immediately after <div> elements
[attribute=value]	[target=_blank]	Selects all elements with target="_blank"
:first-child	p:first-child	Selects every <p> element that is the first child of its parent
:hover	a:hover	Selects links on mouse over

For more see CSS Selectors Reference[10].

---

[10] CSS Selectors Reference: https://phpa.me/w3schools-css-selectors

Responsive CSS

In the early days of the web, screen resolutions did not vary significantly. With the evolution of the web, new devices proliferated, and new screen sizes created new challenges. New strategies were needed to keep websites usable across different device sizes. We call webpages that adapt to different screen sizes, "responsive."

Responsiveness is necessary nowadays. Different devices and varying display resolutions mean you can't assume your webpage is readable or usable with a single, fixed-width design. You can't assume all of your users have 800-pixel devices, for sure. You have to make your website responsive so users can read and interact with it on their phones, tablets, laptops, and other devices. Responsiveness means the elements on your page, menus, sidebars, primary content containers, can reflow intelligently based on the page size available.

Responsive design is more than not just moving elements according to the width. How the grid would break, or which elements would be shown, are the questions you ask. A wide horizontal navigation bar wouldn't work well on a narrower phone display. Small screens usually require simplification of design or different solutions altogether.

Media Queries

When designing a layout, you might get to a moment where some elements must have different style attributes for different screen orientations (landscape versus profile), type (screen or media), measurement (height or width), or some other attribute. Media queries allow you to target CSS rules meeting one or more of those device properties. In practice, this tells the browser on a phone to use different CSS rules than a browser on a high-resolution laptop screen.

To organize your rules, you can distinguish the different styles by placing them in separate style sheets. Within your primary style sheet, use @import to load those specialized files. This is the CSS at-rule. According to MDN web docs, CSS at-rules are:

> "CSS statement that instructs CSS how to behave."- MDN

A typical setup contains our default styles in the main style sheet—you could name it style.css. For custom styles, create another style sheet, for example, small-devices.css. For each target, you can have a unique style sheet.

For example, to configure something to work only for a specific device orientation, we would have something like the following code. It shows a collection of styles only applied to screens reporting a landscape orientation (where the width is larger than the height).

```
@media screen and (orientation: landscape) {
    //…
}
```

Similarly, for printed media, you can use the following query.

```
@media print {
    // …
}
```

Media query syntax works as follows:

```
@media (media type) (logical operator or ,) (rule) (logical operator or ,) ...
```

Keep the following in mind when working for the logical operator:

1. The and operator adds new rules.
2. The , operator combines two rules into one.

The following is a useful starting skeleton for grouping custom selectors for common mobile widths:

```
@media (min-width:320px)  { /* smartphones, iPhone, portrait 480x320 phones */ }
@media (min-width:481px)  { /* portrait e-readers (Nook/Kindle), smaller tablets @ 600
or @ 640 wide. */ }
@media (min-width:641px)  { /* portrait tablets, portrait iPad, landscape e-readers,
landscape 800x480 or 854x480 phones */ }
@media (min-width:961px)  { /* tablet, landscape iPad, lo-res laptops and desktops */ }
@media (min-width:1025px) { /* big landscape tablets, laptops, and desktops */ }
@media (min-width:1281px) { /* hi-res laptops and desktops */ }
```

Layout Strategies

We need to position things on the screen when designing a layout. To do so, we've used various grid strategies based on available browser capabilities to position elements within a web browser. An old way of doing it used table tags (`<table/>`). Table tags are heavy on default styling and are not flexible when it comes to breakpoints, making it harder to work with for layout purposes and custom styling. For these reasons, web designers realized and agreed that HTML tables shouldn't be used for layout purposes. We should only use tables to display tabular content. Typically, this is where you need to show a paginated list of database results.

Through experimentation and perseverance, designers devised tableless layout techniques. Positioning and floats made it possible; however, they are challenging and require a deeper understanding of how different browsers render HTML.

3. CSS Crash Course

One useful example of the tableless approach can be found in this Tableless layout HOWTO[11]. Let's take a look at the following example. In Listing 3.10, we have a three-column layout with the main content flanked by a left and right sidebar.

Listing 3.10

```
 1. :root {
 2.     --common-sidebar-width: 10.2em;
 3.     --common-min-height: 30em;
 4. }
 5.
 6. body {
 7.     margin: 0px;
 8. }
 9.
10. /* Properties that both side lists have in common */
11. div.link-list {
12.     width: var(--common-sidebar-width);
13.     min-height: var(--common-min-height);
14.     position: absolute;
15.     top: 0;
16.     font-size: 80%;
17.     padding-left: 1%;
18.     padding-right: 1%;
19.     margin-left: 0;
20.     margin-right: 0;
21.     border: 1px solid #000;
22. }
23.
24. /* We leave some place on the side using the margin-* properties */
25. #main {
26.     margin-left: var(--common-sidebar-width);
27.     min-height: var(--common-min-height);
28.     margin-right: 10.2em;
29.     padding: 1px 0px;
30.     border: 1px solid #000;
31. }
32.
33. /* And then we put each list on its place */
34. #list1 {
35.     left: 0;
36. }
37.
38. #list2 {
39.     right: 0;
40. }
```

_____

[11] _Tableless layout HOWTO:_ _https://www.w3.org/2002/03/csslayout-howto_

The HTML structure to implement the layout with the above CSS is, at its core, not complicated. Note, we've omitted any actual content—like article titles and paragraphs—which do not affect the basic layout.

```
<div id="main"></div>
<div id="list1" class="link-list"></div>
<div id="list2" class="link-list"></div>
```

The main element comes first, so we don't have the size of the list elements (list1 and list2) interfering with its top positioning. To position this main element in the center, we add a margin to both sides with the width of the list elements of each side. Once those two steps are in place, we position the list elements as absolute and set them on each side with the left:0; for the left one, and right:0 for the right side.

Note that in this example, we are using CSS variables[12], which are relatively new to the web, but are supported by all major browsers except for Internet Explorer. The rendered result looks similar to Figure 3.3.

Figure 3.3. Tableless Layout rendered

I chose to implement three columns here, but this is not a rule. One known problem with this approach is accounting for different screen sizes, such that floating and positioning are not very consistent. It's also difficult to control the vertical alignment of the sidebar and main container.

Tableless layouts are still commonly used, and you are likely to see them in older themes and websites. Nowadays, we have other relevant approaches, and the two most useful are Grid Layout and Flexbox.

Grid Layout

The Grid Layout Module[13] allows layout creation without floating and positioning. It is a solution for two-dimensional layouts. The Grid Layout works similar to tables when it comes to the concept of using rows and columns, but is more flexible. This approach is known as *layout first* —different from Flexbox, which is *content first*. If you need to define your layout as a row and a column simultaneously, Grid Layout is available. Otherwise, if you only need to reflow a row or column of elements, Flexbox is a better option.

This module works with two types of elements: containers and child elements. Any immediate child of a container is considered a grid item.

---

[12] CSS variables: https://phpa.me/mozdev-custom-css-props
[13] Grid Layout Module: https://phpa.me/w3-css-grid

The main elements to consider when using the Grid Layout Module are:

1. Grid Columns: The group of grid cells at the same vertical line.
2. Grid Rows: The group of grid cells at the same horizontal line.
3. Grid Gaps: The space between columns and rows, called "grid gap rows" and "grid gap columns."
4. Grid Lines: The lines between columns and rows, called "grid line rows" and "grid line columns."

To make your grid responsive, you should use CSS Media Queries, covered earlier in this chapter. You should set a different grid disposition setting for specific screen measurements. Unlike the previous technique, with grid, you are not constrained by the order of elements in your HTML document.

To get a basic understanding, let's build a simple Grid Layout showing the power of this module. It starts by following some necessary steps:

1. Add `display: grid` to the container to enable the grid layout module.
2. Use the `grid-template-areas` property for positioning. You can name them as you want, usually based on their purpose, e.g.,
   `grid-template-areas: "sidebar header body";`.
3. Use the `grid-template-columns` property for the number of columns and their sizes. You can use CSS measurement units like px and fr, and this command can be as fragmented as needed, e.g., `grid-template-columns: 60px 60px;`.
4. Consider the 'grid-template-rows' property for the presentation of the rows. This has the same effect as the `grid-template-columns` property, but for the rows.
5. `grid-areas` are the name of the items and their correspondent position, mentioned in the `grid-template-areas`, occupied by the correspondent element. A `grid-area` is responsible for specifying the location of the item in the grid, and, consequently, the size. This is accomplished by referencing the areas defined in the `grid-template`.

Also, note the `grid-area` attribute we added to the specific item. We can use this attribute in two different manners:

1. We can add a reference to which the same name at the `grid-template-areas` point to in the template definition as in Listing 3.11.
2. We can specify it as a shorthand of another group of attributes: `grid-row-start`, `grid-column-start`, `grid-row-end`, `grid-column-end`. The second manner is present in the example of Figure 3.7.

The following example uses the `grid-template` shorthand, which contains all these previous items. The syntax is as follows:

```
grid-template: grid-template-areas grid-template-rows / grid-template-column values
```

Listing 3.11 shows one example.

Listing 3.11

```
 1. .container, .container > div {
 2.     border: 1px solid #000;
 3.     padding: 10px;
 4. }
 5.
 6. .container {
 7.     display: grid;
 8.     grid-template: "a a a" 40px "b c c" 40px "b c c" 40px / 1fr 1fr 1fr;
 9. }
10.
11. .cell-1 {
12.     grid-area: a;
13. }
14.
15. .cell-2 {
16.     grid-area: b;
17. }
18.
19. .cell-3 {
20.     grid-area: c;
21. }
```

To use this layout, our HTML needs the following elements.

```
<div class="container">
    <div class="cell-1"></div>
    <div class="cell-2"></div>
    <div class="cell-3"></div>
</div>
```

The presentation of this is shown in Figure 3.4.

Figure 3.4. Grid Layout Example 1

To add gaps to our previous grid, we can add this line to the .container element as follows.

```
.container {
    grid-gap: 10px;
}
```

This, in the same layout, results in something like Figure 3.5.

Figure 3.5. Grid Layout Example 2

From this point, we can look at a more complex example to see how deep the rabbit hole goes. Imagine a scenario where we need an item to be bigger than the grid's expected height. We could specify one element's height to be bigger than the space set for it.

```
.cell-2 {
    grid-area: b;
    height: 100px;
    background: blue;
}
```

Figure 3.6. Grid Layout Example 3

The result looks something like Figure 3.6.

We might also need to change the order of the elements. For this, we use the properties grid-column-(start/end) and grid-row-(start/end).

In the previous example, we used the grid-template property, which is more generic. It contains other properties within itself. In Listing 3.12, we use a more fragmented approach.

Listing 3.12

```
 1. * {
 2.     box-sizing: border-box;
 3. }
 4.
 5. .container {
 6.     display: grid;
 7.     grid-template-columns: repeat(3, 1fr);
 8.     grid-auto-rows: 100px;
 9.     border: 1px solid #000;
10. }
11.
12. .container > div {
13.     border: 1px solid #000;
14.     padding: 1em;
15. }
16.
17. .cell1 {
18.     grid-column-start: 1;
19.     grid-column-end: 3;
20.     grid-row-start: 1;
21.     grid-row-end: 3;
22. }
23.
24. .cell2 {
25.     grid-column-start: 2;
26.     grid-row-start: 3;
27.     grid-row-end: 5;
28. }
```

The corresponding HTML is shown here.

```
<div class="container">
    <div class="cell1">Cell 1</div>
    <div class="cell2">Cell 2</div>
    <div class="cell3">Cell 3</div>
    <div class="cell4">Cell 4</div>
    <div class="cell5">Cell 5</div>
    <div class="cell6">Cell 6</div>
</div>
```

Figure 3.7 shows what a browser renders.

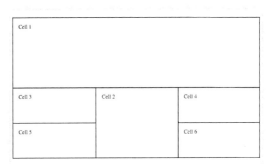

Figure 3.7. Grid Layout Example 4

We could change the order or the cells, placing Cell 2 in the first position of its row, by changing our CSS without editing the HTML.

```
.cell2 {
    grid-column-start: 1;
}
```

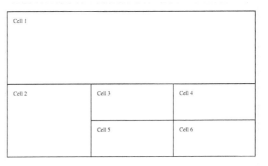

Figure 3.8. Grid Layout Example 5

You should see something like Figure 3.8.

We can make the same type of change to the vertical positioning by adjusting the following property.

```
.cell2 {
    grid-row-start: 1;
    grid-row-end: 5;
    background: blue;
}
```

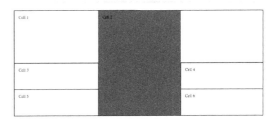

Figure 3.9. Grid Layout Example 6

The browser should render something like Figure 3.9. Notice Cell 2 is now overlapping Cell 1.

As you can see, Grid Layout allows the positioning of areas to be configured without coupling it to the order of elements in the HTML document. For a different approach, where you need to define an element's behavior in a one-dimensional column or row, use Flexbox.

Flexbox

Before we dig into how Flexbox works, we have to understand the normal flow a browser uses to render items. The normal flow is the way elements are rendered relative to each other on the page. Formatting contexts determine this behavior, and the most important contexts are block and inline.

HTML elements come with default properties. One of these properties is the formatting context. The formatting context can change in some situations, and for layout, we have properties like `float`, `position` and `display`. These properties are useful for layout because they affect the block formatting context.

As an example of a block formatting context, we have the cell of the Grid Layout explained in the last section or a `<div>` at its default behavior. In this formatting context, elements are considered boxes laid vertically when not floated, and horizontally when floated and with enough space. There are specific conditions that can cause an item to fall into the block formatting context[14]. There is also the W3C official specification[15].

For the inline formatting context, we have as an example the tag `<i>`. This tag sets the style of a text as italic by default and has the inline formatting context. In this formatting context, elements follow the text flow, appearing as part of the text. One of its unique characteristics is that it ignores the margin-top and margin-bottom attributes. For more information, Mozilla.org[16] provides excellent documentation. You can also read the official inline formatting specification[17].

According to the writing mode[18] of the language, the formatting context can behave differently. We will cover aspects of the English context here, where the block direction is vertical, and the inline direction is horizontal (right-to-left but writing mode isn't concerned with this aspect), as seen in Figure 3.10.

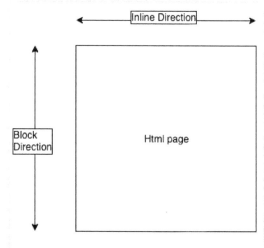

Figure 3.10. Block and Inline directions

[14] block formatting context: https://phpa.me/mozdev-block-context
[15] W3C official specification: https://phpa.me/w3-block-formatting
[16] Mozilla.org: https://phpa.me/mozdev-inline-formatting
[17] inline formatting specification: https://phpa.me/w3-inline-formatting
[18] writing mode: https://www.w3.org/TR/css-writing-modes-3/

The most common container element to use when you need a simple block formatting context is a `<div>` element. The element we once used when we needed a simple inline formatting context is `<span>`. I chose these two to mention because each has some attributes in place. The `<div>` element comes, by default, with the CSS value `display: block`. The `<span>` tag comes with none. These are two tags with the fewest default attributes. You don't have to spend time and memory overriding many default properties. If you want to check other elements and their default properties, you can visit the W3Schools Default CSS Values Page[19]. Make sure to research the HTML tag properties when using them to ensure you use the most appropriate ones.

It is also important to mention that the less you write, the fewer problems you have. If you can avoid writing extra CSS by using an element with the desired default properties in place, use it! Optimal code is always welcome, and it causes the code to be more readable too. Once the HTML elements behave uniformly, new developers should have less trouble understanding how they work.

Flexible Contents

You can activate the Flexbox module in a container element by adding the `display:flex;` property. When that happens, instead of the *normal flow*, you have the *flex-flow*.

The Flexbox[20] layout is a module intended to offload control of how items fill an available space to the browser. It works with two categories of properties: flex containers and flex items. The `display:flex` property is meant for the container elements.

Note that flexmode is for single-direction layouts. It fits better in designs where you have a list of items organized relative to each other. If you need to present items based on rows and columns, grid-layout is the correct option since it allows you to organize layouts based on the grid.

The container has a few other properties listed next.

Container Properties

Align-Items

This attribute specifies the cross-axis alignment for the flex-items inside the current container.

Default: `stretch`. Options: `stretch`, `flex-start`, `flex-end`, `center`, `baseline`.

---

[19] W3Schools Default CSS Values Page: *https://phpa.me/w3schools-css-defaults*
[20] Flexbox: *https://www.w3.org/TR/css-flexbox-1/*

Option	Description
stretch	Stretch the flex-items to fill the container.
flex-start	Based on the cross-axis alignment, place items at the start of it.
flex-end	Based on the cross-axis alignment, place items at the end of it.
center	Based on the cross-axis alignment, place items at the center of it.
baseline	Based on the cross-axis, items are aligned to the text's horizontal line.

In Listing 3.13 and 3.14, we set the item's alignment inside the flex container to be centered vertically.

Listing 3.13

```
1.  .container {
2.      display: flex;
3.      align-items: center;
4.      border: 1px solid #000;
5.      padding: 10px;
6.      height: 100px;
7.  }
8.
9.  .item {
10.     border: 1px solid #000;
11.     padding: 10px;
12. }
13.
14. .item:nth-child(1) {
15.     height: 50px;
16. }
17.
18. .item:nth-child(2) {
19.     height: 20px;
20. }
21.
22. .item:not(:nth-child(1)) {
23.     margin-left: 10px;
24. }
```

Listing 3.14

```
<div class="container">
    <div class="item">
        Item 1
    </div>
    <div class="item">
        Item 2
    </div>
</div>
```

As you can see in Figure 3.11, Item 1 and 2 are vertically aligned at the center.

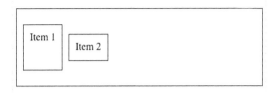

Align-Content

`align-content` defines the item's alignment within the container based on the cross-axis.

Figure 3.11. Flexbox Container - Align Items

It is crucial to notice that the description here assumes `flex-direction: row` (which is the default when we don't set a `flex-direction`).

Option	Description
flex-start	The alignment is set to the top of the container.
flex-end	The alignment is set to the bottom of the container.
center	The alignment is set to the vertical center of the container.
space-between	Items are distributed to occupy the full space by having equal spaces between them. With this set, we have the first item set to the start (top) of the container and the latest item set to the end (bottom) of the container.
space-around	This is the same as space-between, but here we have equal spaces also added between the first item and the top of the container and between the latest item and the bottom of the container.
stretch	Items are stretched to fill the container's space.

Listing 3.15 is an example of the container aligning its items to the bottom through the flex-end parameter set align-content.

Listing 3.15

```
1.  .container {
2.      display: flex;
3.      align-items: flex-end;
4.      border: 1px solid #000;
5.      padding: 10px;
6.      height: 100px;
7.  }
8.
9.  .item {
10.     border: 1px solid #000;
11.     padding: 10px;
12. }
```

```
13.
14. .item:not(:nth-child(1)) {
15.     margin-left: 10px;
16. }
17.
18. .item:nth-child(1) {
19.     height: 50px;
20. }
21.
22. .item:nth-child(2) {
23.     height: 30px;
24. }
```

In Listing 3.16, we have the two items inside the container set to flex.

Listing 3.16

```
<div class="container">
    <div class="item">
        Item 1
    </div>
    <div class="item">
        Item 2
    </div>
</div>
```

Figure 3.12. Flexbox Container - Align Content

In Figure 3.12, we see the items getting aligned to the end of the container.

Flex-Direction

The main axis of the flex container is affected by the flex-direction attribute. It defines the direction of the flex-items within this container. As we mentioned before, Flexbox is a single-direction layout, and this attribute sets which direction they will follow on its main axis while getting organized.

Option	Description
row	This sets the flex-items to follow the inline direction of the "writing-mode." E.g., when in Latin-based systems, it is left to right.
row-reverse	This is the reverse of "row."
column	This is the same as "row," but it follows the "block-direction" of the "writing-mode." E.g., this is set from top to bottom when in Latin-based systems.
column-reverse	This is the reverse of the "column."

Here (Listing 3.17) we have the `flex-direction` attribute set to "row" at the flex-container element (the CSS selector `.container`).

Listing 3.17

```
1. .container {
2.     display: flex;
3.     flex-direction: row;
4.     border: 1px solid #000;
5.     padding: 10px;
6. }
7.
8. .item {
9.     border: 1px solid #000;
10.    padding: 10px;
11. }
12.
13. .item:not(:nth-child(1)) {
14.     margin-left: 10px;
15. }
```

In Listing 3.18, we have two flex-items inside the flex-container marked with the class `container`.

Listing 3.18

```
<div class="container">
    <div class="item">
        Item 1
    </div>
    <div class="item">
        Item 2
    </div>
</div>
```

Figure 3.13. Flexbox Container - Flex Direction

In Figure 3.13, we see the result of the code snippets above, where the flex container is affected by the `flex-direction: row`, in a Latin-based system with the "writing-mode" `ltr` (left-to-right).

Flex-Wrap

This attribute sets whether items are forced into multiple lines when there is not enough space ("wrapped"). It also sets the direction of the wrap. It is important to note, it is also affected by the `flex-direction` attribute when it comes to defining the "cross-start" and "cross-end."

Option	Description
nowrap	Keeps flex-items laid out in a single line. Forces an overflow of the flex-container if the flex-items width is larger than the flex-container's width.
wrap	Forces flex-items into multiple lines when their width is larger than the flex-container's width.
wrap-reverse	This is the same as wrap, but the "cross-start" and the "cross-end" are permuted, reversing the flex-direction influence.

Here we have the flex-container with the flex-wrap set to "wrap-reverse." (Listing 3.19)

Listing 3.19

```
1. .container {
2.     display: flex;
3.     flex-wrap: wrap-reverse;
4.     border: 1px solid #000;
5.     padding: 10px;
6.     width: 200px;
7. }
8.
9. .item {
10.     border: 1px solid #000;
11.     padding: 10px;
12.     width: 80px;
13. }
```

Listing 3.20 has three items inside a container.

Listing 3.20

```
1. <div class="container">
2.     <div class="item">
3.         Item 1
4.     </div>
5.     <div class="item">
6.         Item 2
7.     </div>
8.     <div class="item">
9.         Item 3
10.     </div>
11. </div>
```

In the following image (Figure 3.14), we can see how the flex-items are affected by the flex-wrap: wrap-reverse. Even though items are listed in numeric order, the wrap-reverse changed the direction of the wrapped items.

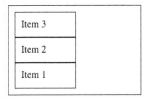

Justify-Content

Figure 3.14. Flexbox Container - Flex Wrap

The justify-content attribute sets how the distribution of items happens inside the container. They are affected relative to the main-axis when the container is "flex." This attribute also can be set to "grid containers," when so, it affects items relative to the "inline-axis." It can set spaces around or between the items within the container.

Option	Description
flex-start	Items are pushed towards the "line-start" of the container's main axis.
flex-end	Items are pushed towards the "line-end" of the container's main axis.
center	Pushes items towards the center of the container's main axis.
space-between	Sets the first item to the start of the line, the last item to the end of the line, and evenly distributes all other items in the container with equal spaces in between.
space-around	Items are evenly distributed in the container's main axis, with equal space around each.
space-evenly	Items are evenly distributed in the container's main axis, with all the spaces between items being equal. Unlike the space-around parameter, the space is considered by itself, while in the space-around the space is "the space around the items," which causes the space to be smaller at the edges.

Here we have the justify-content: space-around set to the flex container, see Listing 3.21.

Listing 3.21

```
1. .container {
2.     display: flex;
3.     justify-content: space-around;
4.     border: 1px solid #000;
5.     padding: 10px;
6. }
```

```
 7.
 8. .item {
 9.     border: 1px solid #000;
10.     padding: 10px;
11. }
12.
13. .item:not(:nth-child(1)) {
14.     margin-left: 10px;
15. }
```

At the HTML code shown in Listing 3.22, we have two items inside a container.

Listing 3.22

```
<div class="container">
    <div class="item">
        Item 1
    </div>
    <div class="item">`
        Item 2
    </div>
</div>
```

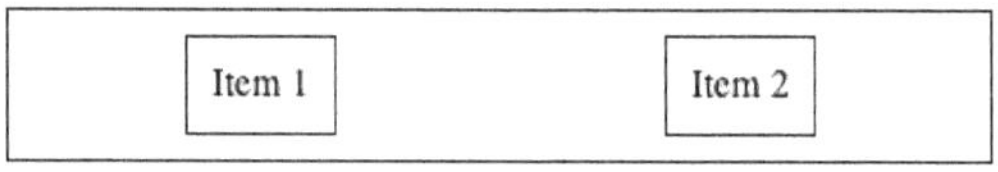

Figure 3.15. Flexbox Container - Justify Content

Figure 3.15 shows the space around the flex-items being equal. Notice that the space at the edges is smaller than the space in between. For all those spaces to be equal, use the option justify-content: space-evenly.

Item Properties

Order

Flex items are rendered in the same order as they occur in the HTML code. If needed, we can reorder flex items by using the order attribute. This attribute belongs in the flex-item selector. You set the number (starting with one) for the item's disposition as a value for this attribute, e.g., if you have three things, and you want the first HTML item to appear second, you need to set it to order: 2.

In Listing 3.23, we have the order: n attribute set to each flex-item.

Listing 3.23

```
1. .container {
2.     display: flex;
3.     border: 1px solid #000;
4.     padding: 10px;
5. }
```

```
 6.
 7. .item {
 8.     border: 1px solid #000;
 9.     padding: 10px;
10. }
11.
12. .item:nth-child(1) {
13.     order: 3;
14. }
15.
16. .item:nth-child(2) {
17.     order: 4;
18. }
19.
20. .item:nth-child(3) {
21.     order: 1;
22. }
23.
24. .item:nth-child(4) {
25.     order: 2;
26. }
27.
28. .item:not(:nth-child(3)) {
29.     margin-left: 10px;
30. }
```

This HTML code (Listing 3.24) has four items inside a container.

Listing 3.24

```
 1. <div class="container">
 2.     <div class="item">
 3.         Item 1
 4.     </div>
 5.     <div class="item">
 6.         Item 2
 7.     </div>
 8.     <div class="item">
 9.         Item 3
10.     </div>
11.     <div class="item">
12.         Item 4
13.     </div>
14. </div>
```

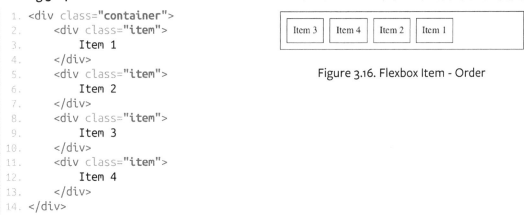

Figure 3.16. Flexbox Item - Order

Figure 3.16 shows the result of the reordering done by the order attribute. Item 3 is set to position 1, Item 4 for position 2, Item 2 set to position 3, and Item 1 set to position 4.

Flex-Grow

This attribute defines how much each item grows according to the container's proportion. If you have two items, and both items are set to `flex-grow: 1`, both equally grow when the space available grows. However, if we set one to `flex-grow: 2` and the other to `flex-grow: 1`, the first one grows twice as much.

In Listing 3.25, we have the flex-item 1 set to `grow: 1`, and flex-item 2 is set to `grow: 2`.

Listing 3.25

```
1.  .container {
2.      display: flex;
3.      border: 1px solid #000;
4.      padding: 10px;
5.  }
6.
7.  .item {
8.      border: 1px solid #000;
9.      padding: 10px;
10.     flex-grow: 1;
11. }
12.
13. .item:not(:nth-child(1)) {
14.     margin-left: 10px;
15. }
16.
17. .item:nth-child(2) {
18.     flex-grow: 2;
19. }
```

Here we have two items inside a container. (Listing 3.26)

Listing 3.26

```
<div class="container">
    <div class="item">
        Item 1
    </div>
    <div class="item">
        Item 2
    </div>
</div>
```

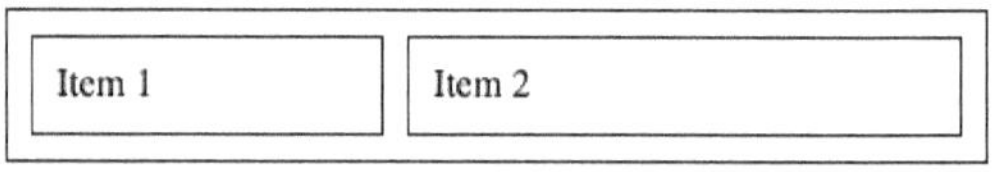

Figure 3.17. Flexbox Item - Flex Grow

In Figure 3.17, we see the result, where the flex-item 2 grows the double of the flex-item 1.

Flex-Shrink And Flex-Basis

We describe these two elements together because flex-shrink depends on flex-basis.

Flex shrink defines how proportionally items shrink when there is not enough space within the container element. Here you set the number of how proportionally the item shrinks.

Flex basis defines the base width of the item when the container's width changes. This is the width measurement, and we can express it in any valid CSS unit (e.g., px, em, and so on).

In Listing 3.27, we have attributes specifying how the items grow (flex-grow) and shrink (flex-shrink), and also its base width (flex-basis).

Listing 3.27

```
1. .container {
2.     display: flex;
3.     border: 1px solid #000;
4.     padding: 10px;
5.     box-sizing: border-box;
6. }
7.
8. .item {
9.     border: 1px solid #000;
10.    padding: 10px;
11.    flex-grow: 1;
12.    flex-shrink: 1;
13.    flex-basis: 20em;
14. }
15.
16. .item:not(:nth-child(1)) {
17.    margin-left: 10px;
18. }
19.
20. .item:nth-child(2) {
21.    flex-shrink: 13;
22. }
```

The HTML code in Listing 3.28 has two items inside a container.

Listing 3.28

```
<div class="container">
    <div class="item">
        Item 1
    </div>
    <div class="item">
        Item 2
    </div>
</div>
```

Figure 3.18 shows items layout when there is more than enough space.

Figure 3.19 shows the resulting layout when there is not enough space.

For an engaging way to learn Flexbox by practicing, see Flexbox Froggy[21].

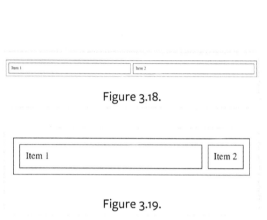

Figure 3.18.

Figure 3.19.

Conclusion

With these in hand, you are prepared to build modern and flexible HTML pages. One final observation is to be aware of the browser support for the CSS properties you use. As new CSS modules are proposed, browsers like Google Chrome, Mozilla Firefox, and Apple's Safari browser may not add support for a new module at the same time. For example, see this page, which enumerates the browser support for the Flexbox module[22] across browsers (Figure 3.20).

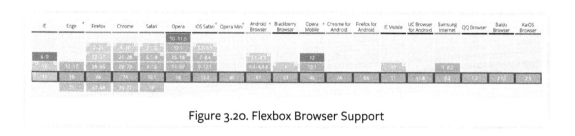

Figure 3.20. Flexbox Browser Support

---

[21] Flexbox Froggy: http://flexboxfroggy.com
[22] Flexbox module: https://caniuse.com/#feat=flexbox

Chapter

4

The Gutenberg Editor

Gutenberg is a whole new way of writing. The workflow is not 100% unique; we have a mix of page builder adn WYSIWYG editor. Some WordPress plugins on the web, such as Elementor or Page Builder by SiteOrigin, have offered a similar editing experience. In this case, the product is a simple blog post or a complex webpage.

The Block Editor

You can check out the new editor experience at https://testgutenberg.com.

While we can say the block editor is a type of page builder, it is more than that. The differences mirror the innovation of the original Gutenberg printing press created in the 15th century. Back then, text blocks were produced manually. Someone would have to copy the text by hand when they wanted to reuse or reproduce the text. We find the same thing in the current workflow of blogs/websites. Similar chunks of content are reused very often across multiple pages. Updating all the instances of that content can be painful if you've simply copy-and-pasted them to different pages.

What Does It Do?

What makes Gutenberg innovative is its use of the block and what it can accomplish. The block editor makes available advanced features such as cover images with immediate preview, tons of embedding options, paragraphs drag-and-drop, advanced layout editing, creation of templates with groups of blocks, etc.

Editing Blocks

With the old editor, we could write content in the WYSIWYG editor, specify the post attributes at the metaboxes and save it. This workflow is still there. However, when you are writing the content in the Gutenberg editor, and type "enter," you not only advance to the next paragraph but also add a "block paragraph." By default, the editor adds a paragraph block, but that could be another type between the tons already available.

Each available block accomplishes a different goal, and the elevated UX is a big selling point. In addition to the basics, blocks can be more complex, like a carousel of images or embedded videos. As mentioned earlier, blocks are like an advanced shortcode. They can have very advanced functionality that goes from a simple paragraph to a complex form that, once submitted, makes an asynchronous request to a separate server and retrieves useful information. There are likely other features available on the frontend, depending upon the type of block in use. Unfortunately, blocks are still in development, and it might take a while to have a large variety of useful and stable blocks available.

Using shortcodes has not traditionally been very user-friendly for editors, resulting in post content mixed with code. By having two rendering modes, blocks allow developers to use one display when editing a block and another to preview the final content. For example, while editing an image, users will see a form to pick media and specify how it should display. Then, as soon as an image gets selected and the user moves to edit another block, they see the image block's image preview. That is a huge step forward when it comes to the UX; the user can now immediately see how things will look. Previously, we had to review anything more complex than simple text on the front end after saving the post. There's a certain amount of risk involved with this type of workflow, such as publishing a post prematurely.

Block Reuse

We can reuse blocks, saving significant time and effort for specific cases. Let's take a look at an example.

Imagine you have a document reused across many of your blog posts. This document has a description and an image. If, after making five of those occurrences, you need to update the image in one, you have to update all the others manually. Doing so assumes you know or track where it's used in the first place.

With blocks, you save time on tasks like this. You can define blocks once, and save that occurrence as a reusable block. When you want to use it again in a new post, you add it in.

Block Editor Workflows—Build A Page

Let's build a page with a block to understand the advanced features better this new editor offers. Let's prepare an advanced page template using the new Block Editor.

Figure 4.1. Document Context

Contexts

To begin, when using Gutenberg, you have two contexts: the post context and the block context. On the Gutenberg screen, you should see something similar to Figure 4.1 and Figure 4.2.

Figure 4.2. Block Context

The post context is the context when you don't have any block selected. In this context, in a default WordPress installation, you have a sidebar with two tabs: Document and Block. You should be in the Document tab. Here you'll see some options for the post visibility and authoring. In collapsed options above, you find Permalink, Categories, Tags, Excerpt, and Discussion. Each of these is a meta box from the Classic Editor; they work the same here.

By not having any block selected, if you go to the Block tab in the sidebar, you will see a message "No block selected." If you happen to choose a block, you'll see that block's options; the image above the block context shows the paragraph block options.

Paragraph Block

As an example of Gutenberg's usage, we will customize our paragraph block according to a few options. We can set the first letter of this paragraph to be larger by toggling the Drop Cap option, as shown in Figure 4.3.

Another interesting option is the color palette available for this paragraph block. Depending on the theme that you have installed, this option might change, showing colors closer to your site colors. This doesn't keep you from selecting more colors, which are available in the Custom Color Picker (see Figure 4.4).

There is also a nice feature that points out when you are choosing colors that might be a problem for your content's visual accessibility. You might have a combination of colors without sufficient contrast or might be problematic for visitors with some forms of color blindness. When that happens, you should see something similar to Figure 4.5.

Figure 4.3. Drop Cap option

Figure 4.4. Color Palettes

Figure 4.5. Color Palettes accessibility alert

After setting a color for one paragraph and leaving the other paragraph with the default color, we should see something like in Figure 4.6.

Image Block

To see another example of what this new editor is capable of, let's add an image to our post. To start, add a new block of the type "image" (see Figure 4.7).

As with the paragraph blocks, you have options on the toolbar and the sidebar of the editor.

In Figure 4.8, you can see the toolbar.

Here you have the positioning options as well as the ability to convert to other block types. The image icon with the caret down shows what you can convert this block to. This conversion is done based on the similarities of the blocks (you can only convert blocks to similar blocks), and for every new block developed, this support needs to be pointed and added at the development stage. Hence, the system identifies the new block as similar to existing ones. By default, you can convert this image block to other similar blocks that can use this block's data; that would be a gallery, cover, file, media, and text.

Figure 4.6. Paragraphs at the frontend

Figure 4.7. Adding image block

Figure 4.8. Image Block Toolbar

The image block options at the sidebar might change through time, but, for WordPress 5.1, they are (see Figure 4.9) for the theme Twenty Nineteen.

- **Alternative Text**: You can change the alternative text that will be shown or read when it comes to accessibility. It should be descriptive of the image's contents.
- **Image Size**: This defines how big the image is when rendered on the page. You might select the size having in mind the style of the presentation you need and the performance you want. Selecting smaller sizes causes WordPress to use smaller images storage wise and smaller files download quicker too.
- **Image Dimensions**: You can specify the width and the height, but be careful not to break the original aspect ratio to keep the image at its best quality.
- **Link Settings**: Here, you can select if the link to the image is an attachment (to send the user to a media post page) or if it is media (to present it in another tab with only the image—outside of WordPress).
- **Advanced** (Additional CSS Class): You can specify a custom CSS style to your image block, making it present differently or even add some effects (e.g., to start transparent and to get its opacity increased when hovered)

Figure 4.9

Figure 4.10. Image block at the frontend

If the image fails to load for any reason, a browser might show the size of the presented image, the link, and any additional CSS.

As an example, we can change the size of the source image to a thumbnail. However, that would degrade the resolution if the positioning at the toolbar specifies the image is full width and WordPress upscales the image. Don't be afraid to experiment to better grasp the implications of the attributes.

If we just keep the positioning at the toolbar to full width and keep the size as full size, Figure 4.10 shows what that looks like.

If this image is the first, we might want this block to be a cover instead of a simple block between paragraphs. Covers are the wide images used to start sections, or even to start the post or page itself. For that purpose, you can add text to it, that will show up in the front of the image. If so, we can change this image block to a cover block. To do this, we must move this block to the top with the controls available on the left side of the block. See Figure 4.11.

Once this block is first, we will convert it to a cover block, see Figure 4.12.

This cover block gives us some other options, as seen in Figure 4.13.

Figure 4.11. Moving image block up

Figure 4.12. Converting an Image Block to a Cover Block

Figure 4.13. Cover Block options

We will select the full-width option (see Figure 4.14).

For the cover block, we can also add a label (see Figure 4.15).

The result on the frontend should be something like we see in Figure 4.16.

Figure 4.14. Turning Cover Block to Full Width

Document Context

As mentioned in the Contexts section, the document context is the post editor's sidebar, where we set attributes for the entire document. Things we can manage there are:

Figure 4.15. Adding a label to Cover Block

- **Status & Visibility**: select if the post will be published, private or password protected. You can also pick a date for this post to be published.
- **Permalinks**: here, you select how the URL looks for the current post. You can choose an unused slug.
- **Categories**: choose a category for the current post—helpful for organization and filtering.
- **Tags**: select the tags for the current post. It has the same purpose as categories and serves as metadata for the post, which improves searchability.
- **Featured Image**: this is usually the image presented as a thumbnail of the post when such opportunity happens, e.g., posts lists with thumbnails.
- **Excerpt**: This is a small description of the post, where we can say in a few words the content of the post.

Figure 4.16. Cover Block front end

This list can grow depending on the metaboxes you have available in your WordPress installation. For our post, we want to confirm that privacy is set to the public. Also, set "Post Templates" in the categories section. In the tags section, check the option "cover" and add some text for the excerpt.

After confirming these things in our sidebar, you should have something like in Figure 4.17.

This is not that different from the Classic Editor when it comes to the basic functionalities, but from these small actions, we can understand the new direction. The changes that resulted in the new UX, also opened WordPress to a new range of authoring possibilities available now because of the new way to interact with the editor.

Gutenberg's Origin

Matt Mullenweg announced Gutenberg at the end of 2018 on his blog[1]. He wanted a new default editor experience to be a part of WordPress 5.0. Mullenweg called for a more visual editor, which would allow content editors to create complex layouts without understanding the underlying CSS and HTML. This announcement did not come without pushback from the community. There was a risk that Gutenberg would break many existing plugins, themes, and websites. Gutenberg's development also did not prioritize accessibility so that it could be used effectively by all content editors.

Figure 4.17. Document's scope options

---

[1]   his blog: https://ma.tt/2018/11/a-gutenberg-faq/

Changing the creation experience is, indeed, a bold task because more than 30% of the web now relies on WordPress. This move affected everyone that wanted to keep their sites updated. Because Gutenberg is now the default editor, you need a plugin to use what's now called the Classic Editor[2] to keep the previous editing experience.

Ten years ago, WordPress was already very popular. Even then, WordPress was very innovative, which is one of the many reasons for its popularity. The way WordPress projects put together the most popular web technologies available helped small businesses to succeed. The plugin-based architecture took web development to the next level by allowing the WordPress community to extend its functionality and share the solutions. The Classic Editor's "Edit Post" screen gave the perfect balance for the minimum number of mouse clicks for efficiency. What will Gutenberg be known for?

Information about Gutenberg can be found at https://wordpress.org/gutenberg.

What's New And Improved

Gutenberg is the default editor since WordPress 5.0. The Block Editor builds every single feature possible in the post; you just need to select a block for that purpose. Every block has two different layers: the frontend and the backend. The backend layer offers the form for adding the information required by the block functionality to work on the frontend layer. All of it happens using React at the JS side, but it is all defined via PHP so developers can keep it simple. It may be limited in what it can do, but the trade-off is that backend developers don't have to know much about ReactJS.

When not talking about the visual, the innovations are:

- The Markup
- Reusability of the blocks
- Block templates

The Classic Editor was a basic WYSIWYG editor using raw HTML for content structure. The first thing to notice is the block structure that we have now. The HTML looks like this for the Classic Editor:

```
<p>Welcome to the world of blocks.</p>
```

And like this for Gutenberg:

```
<!-- wp:paragraph {"key": "value"} -->
<p>Welcome to the world of blocks.</p>
<!-- /wp:paragraph -->
```

---

[2]   Classic Editor: https://wordpress.org/plugins/classic-editor/

This is an example of a purely dynamic block markup:

```
<!-- wp:latest-posts {"postsToShow":4,"displayPostDate":true} /-->
```

As you can see, there is additional metadata provided through HTML comments, where data is kept, a type of "meta code." This data is the key to the unique element of this editor. However, it might cause problems when you are bouncing between the two content editors.

It's the structure behind what comes next. Think of blocks as advanced shortcodes. That said, each block can handle functionalities as extensible as any shortcode, but with a better User Experience for content editors.

Blocks are also reusable once prepared. For example, you could write a paragraph about your company, and use that same paragraph on different pages. If you ever change that paragraph in one place, it will update everywhere you used that block.

The structure can get as complex as it needs. That said, if you need to move a bigger chunk of blocks forward, it is possible through the templating process, where you add a "meta block," which organizes and helps structure the content, that can be built by pure text, digital assets, or other blocks.

Building A Block

Let's build a simple block, where the user can add simple rich text with limited options. As you will see, block creation can occur in as few as two steps.

Before we start building it, it is important to mention the official WordPress documentation[3] is an excellent reference.

For this example, we're keeping things simple, so we're not going to look too deeply at JavaScript, and stick with ES5 (ECMAScript 5). React JS is the direction that the community is going now, but even React JS is writable in ES5. This decision will keep our environment simple enough to be customizable by anyone that knows some JavaScript. If you want a more in-depth look at developing with React JS[4], visit the official website.

Preparation

The basic workflow for building blocks utilizes Javascript and PHP. The first uses libraries offered by the WordPress platform to accomplish the functionalities needed to build a block and make it work with Gutenberg. The PHP part registers that script, so the CMS knows what to do and when to do it.

There are a few steps to accomplish your first block. The first is to create a plugin for which you can find more detailed information in the Plugin Development Chapter.

---

[3]   *WordPress documentation: https://wordpress.org/gutenberg/handbook*
[4]   *React JS: https://reactjs.org*

Create a directory at `wp-content/plugins/` called `wp-dev-depth-block`. There, create a file with the name `wp-dev-depth-block.php`, with the following content:

```php
<?php
/**
 * Plugin Name: WT Dev Depth Block
 */
```

That's it! You have a plugin to customize at will! There is one thing to point here though, the plugin might be vulnerable with such a rudimentary implementation of this. Take a look at security practices to ensure you have a basic understanding of how to avoid common problems.

Step One: Register The Block Script

The first step is to register a script to be enqueued on your site. This script defines the block's behavior, setting the dynamic attributes such as the data handled by the block and the processing for that data. During this step, we also register a block type. For that, we hook into the `init` to add the block script and the block register. Add it to the `wp-dev-depth-block.php` file; it should look like Listing 4.1.

Listing 4.1

```php
1.  <?php
2.  /**
3.   * Plugin Name: WT Dev Depth Block
4.   */
5.
6.  if (!defined('WPDDB_PROMOTION_BLOCK_SCRIPT')) {
7.      define('WPDDB_PROMOTION_BLOCK_SCRIPT', 'wpddb-promotion');
8.  }
9.
10. function wpddb_block_init()
11. {
12.     wp_register_script(
13.         WPDDB_PROMOTION_BLOCK_SCRIPT, // the name of our block script
14.         plugins_url('block.js', __FILE__), // the javascript to be enqueued
15.         ['wp-blocks', 'wp-element', 'wp-editor'] // dependencies
16.     );
17.
18.     register_block_type('wpddb/promotion', [
19.         'editor_script' => WPDDB_PROMOTION_BLOCK_SCRIPT,
20.     ]);
21. }
22.
23. add_action('init', 'wpddb_block_init');
```

There are two things here we need to take a closer look at:

1. The `wp_register_script()` is a function that registers the block script, so WordPress knows which script to run while building it. We name the script `wpdb-promotion`—we used the constant `WPDDB_PROMOTION_BLOCK_SCRIPT`. This name will be used again at the block type registration right after the `register_block_type()` function—the use of constants here, as we are using, was convenient. We can use the constant while the actual string can be changed if needed in one place.

2. The third argument of the function `wp_register_script()` is an array with a list of dependencies. These dependencies are WordPress packages available for WordPress development.

Step Two: Prepare The Block Script Structure

We need to pay attention to a few different items that work together to build a successful block:

1. The elements (based on the dependencies) you need to accomplish your goals;

2. the block type object attributes, where you will declare methods like `edit()` and `save()` which are essential for our case here; and

3. the attributes your block will carry, like `string`, `array`, and other types[5].

Now that we have enqueued the JavaScript, we prepare our Javascript code in the file `block.js` as in Listing 4.2

Listing 4.2

```
1. var wpddb = {}
2. wpddb.contentTag = 'p';
3. wpddb.contentClass = 'wpddb-content';
4.
5. (function (blocks, editor, element) {
6.     var el = wp.element.createElement;
7.     var RichText = editor.RichText;
8.
9.     blocks.registerBlockType('wpddb/promotion', {
10.         title: 'WPDDB Promotion',
11.         icon: 'universal-access-alt',
12.         category: 'layout',
13.
14.         attributes: {
15.             content: {
16.                 type: 'array',
17.                 source: 'children',
```

---

[5] types: https://phpa.me/wpdev-block-attributes

```
18.                   selector: '.' + wpddb.contentClass, // using specific selector
19.               },
20.           },
21.
22.       edit: function (props) {
23.           var content = props.attributes.content;
24.
25.           function onChangeContent(newContent) {
26.               props.setAttributes({content: newContent});
27.           }
28.
29.           return el(
30.               'div',
31.               {},
32.               [
33.                   el('h1', {
34.                       key: 'heading1',
35.                   }, 'Back end'),
36.                   el(
37.                       RichText,
38.                       {
39.                           tagName: wpddb.contentTag,
40.                           value: content,
41.                           onChange: onChangeContent,
42.                           className: wpddb.contentClass,
43.                           key: 'body1',
44.                       }
45.                   )
46.               ]
47.           );
48.       },
49.       save: function (props) {
50.           return el(
51.               'div',
52.               {tagName: wpddb.contentTag},
53.               [
54.                   el('h1', {key: 'heading1'}, 'Front end.'),
55.                   el(RichText.Content, {
56.                       value: props.attributes.content,
57.                       className: wpddb.contentClass,
58.                       key: 'body1',
59.                   })
60.               ]
61.           );
62.       },
63.   });
64. }(
65.   window.wp.blocks,
66.   window.wp.blockEditor,
67.   window.wp.element,
68. ));
```

That's it; you have your first WordPress Gutenberg block! This block is editable, scalable, and reusable.

Important topics to take note of with this code:

1. `wpddb.contentClass` was created to keep the name the same through different spots in the code. If they get out of sync, the block breaks. This error happens because we are using the `attributes` attribute, at the second parameter of the `blocks.registerBlockType`, a selector based on the class.

   Tags are used because blocks are usually small. Using class selectors is a better practice than using tags. When your block becomes more complex, the selector might be used when other similar tags carry different data.

2. A tag `h1` was added to the save and edit methods. That tag is not editable. We added this element to show the different parts of the editing experience:

   B   I   ABC   ⋮

   Back end

   my awesome content!

   Figure 4.18

   1. Edits occur in the backend of the Gutenberg editor. You edit your content here, so the elements should have input fields. For this sample block, you should see something similar to Figure 4.18.

   2. The "save" button is visible at the frontend. When you open the post at the public page of your WordPress site, you see this part rendered. Figure 4.19 shows what is visible there.

   Front end

   my awesome content!

   Figure 4.19

3. The line `var el = wp.element.createElement;` makes the "createElement" from the React library available to us. It is used to create elements dynamically. For deeper levels of customization, please refer to the React docs for `createElement()`[6].

The third step would be to customize at will. This workflow is an example of the core process of creating a WordPress block. Congratulations, now you are a Gutenberg Block developer!

---

[6] `createElement()`: *https://phpa.me/reactjs-create-element*

Reusing A Block

Now that we have written and customized a post and created a block, we might want to reuse it across multiple posts. If you are a blogger, and some of your posts share the same structure, or, at least, some chunks of content, this will be useful to you. Before Gutenberg, we would usually accomplish this via shortcodes.

> *The reusability echoes the Gutenberg printing presses from the 16th century. They used organized blocks of text to print copies.*

Creating Reusable Content

To begin, we create a chunk of code with pre-written content, so the next time we use it, we can simply customize the text, keeping the structure. For the first step, you only need to write some text. You can see an example in Figure 4.20.

In the menu, there's an option to change the state of the current block to a "reusable block." When you click on it, you can give it a name, as you can see in Figures 4.21 and 4.22.

Now, you have a reusable block available to add wherever you want. To check this, you can add it again in the next paragraph, as shown in Figures 4.23 and 4.24.

Figure 4.20. Ttext about to become a reusable block

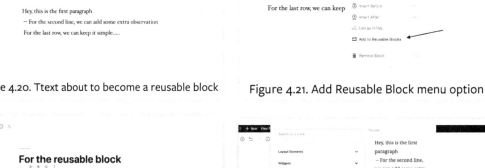

Figure 4.21. Add Reusable Block menu option

Figure 4.22. Reusable block name input

Figure 4.23. Reusable blocks menu with our block

When you change the text after clicking the "edit" button, your reusable block is updated everywhere. It's a handy thing when you want to keep specific information consistent in multiple locations.

A Reusable Template

To manage your created blocks, you can navigate to the "Manage all reusable blocks" section. There, you will see all of the reusable blocks you've created. You should see a screen similar to Figure 4.25.

You can also create a reusable block from here. When you do so, you can create an entire text, with multiple blocks, which allows you to build entire templates. Figure 4.26 shows a template for our reusable block with various blocks.

If you add it to a post, you see something like Figure 4.27 showing a reusable block with multiple blocks added to it.

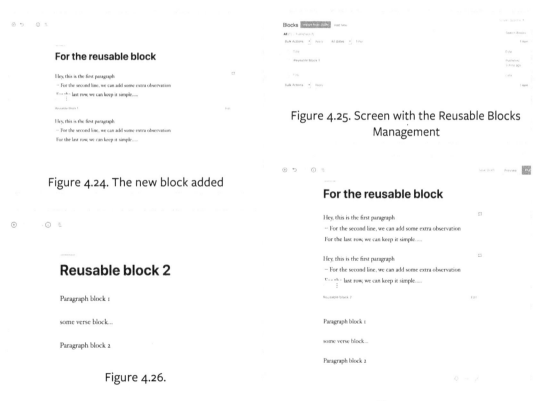

Figure 4.25. Screen with the Reusable Blocks Management

Figure 4.24. The new block added

Figure 4.26.

Figure 4.27.

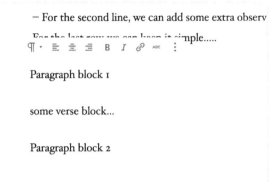

Figure 4.28. Option to convert to regular blocks

Figure 4.29. Reusable block converted to regular blocks

Here, you can convert this to a standard group of blocks again (you have the same option as the regular reusable blocks). If you do so, the changes you make here won't appear in the other copies of this template. The option shown is like Figure 4.28.

Figure 4.29 shows how it would be after converting it.

With these resources available, the WordPress editor becomes much more powerful.

When To Use Gutenberg

There are two main concerns to consider when deciding whether to use Gutenberg.

1. Existing sites
2. Accessibility needed by the site admin/editor

Users have the option to use the Classic Editor instead of Gutenberg if they desire. When it comes to legacy sites, the block editor might not support existing functionalities. It might be due to how your content was prepared or might be due to plugins or themes lacking support by Gutenberg. If you are in one of these categories, it might be better to skip Gutenberg until your plugins and theme support it. If you want to start using Gutenberg, you might need to update or find new plugins to replicate existing functionality.

When it comes to accessibility, you need to evaluate the block editor for its technical accessibility for touch screens and mice. Keyboard navigation and assistive technologies like voice control tools, and even other modalities, might not offer the same experience as the Classic Editor.

In any case, make sure to assess how Gutenberg works in a development environment before deploying these changes to your real website.

Chapter

5

Plugin Development

Having written a few plugins, I have learned a lot about writing them well and in a secure way. So some of what I have learned over the last few years will be imparted to you here. I'm still learning and gaining new insights into what a useful plugin should look like and how it should respect its environments on both the admin and public sides.

Let's start with a few of the ground rules and then look at the coding aspects of this process. Keep in mind there are two major development bases. The first, WordPress, has a lot of its built-in functions that you should consider first. The second is PHP itself, the programming language on which WordPress is based. The PHP ecosystem can provide generalized solutions you can adapt for use on your site. These are usually integrations with other services, APIs, and frameworks.

This chapter is our first more profound look into programming—more so than the rest of the book. If you have no interest in writing code, perhaps this chapter will whet your appetite. It's often a desire to improve a product in which you see flaws. It may follow that as you see flawed plugins, you can fix the code yourself, or create a new plugin from scratch which solves the same issue but more logically and efficiently.

Preparation, Rules, Best Practices

Next, we want to look at practices we should follow when building a plugin to ensure that it is maintainable, secure, and doesn't break your site. In list format, they are as follows.

1. Don't Mess with the WordPress Core.
2. Keep your code separate from other plugins you may be developing, even if they are complementary.
3. Use the WordPress API functions whenever possible; they save time and are native.
4. Prefix your code and tables with unique identifiers to avoid naming collisions.
5. Use object-oriented programming (OOP) whenever possible.
6. Follow secure coding guidelines.
7. Don't use sessions if possible.
8. Use WordPress functions instead of PHP functions.
9. Always use the WordPress Database API when interacting with the database.

Rule One: Don't Mess With The WordPress Core!

Emblazon this rule on your forehead and heart! The core of WordPress is the foundation of the whole website structure well beyond your plugin. If you ever make a change to the core files, you endanger your plugin work and your website's very foundation. Not only do you jeopardize your site, but on the off chance that your core code alterations work out, the risk of instability returns when a new version of WordPress is released. When fixes or enhancements are added to the core codebase of WordPress, you will be out of step with it and, in fact, may even conflict with it. Updates will be a pain if they can be done at all, and your plugin may have to be adjusted with much work to get it realigned. **So, don't mess with the WordPress core!**

Rule Two: Keep Your Code Separate

Keep your plugin code separate from other plugins and keep theme customizations in a distinct child theme. This habit helps with potential conflicts and keeps your code from being dependent on code that may not be defined or installed by a user. It allows each plugin to be 100% independent and helps ensure it can stand and execute independently. Even if you are creating a plugin that augments another one, you should still keep the source code of each one separate as there is no guarantee an end-user will install the same code you may be depending on. Additionally, if you are creating a plugin dependant on another plugin (e.g., one that extends WooCommerce), be sure to check this out as a way to test a dependant plugin exists[1]. Where your code does depend on another plugin or library, document that dependency.

Rule Three: Use WordPress API Functions

Using the functions already provided by WordPress saves time and effort because you are using tried and tested solutions. You are not reinventing the wheel with code that needs to be reviewed and vetted. It saves you time and mental processing cycles by letting you focus on solving the problem at hand. See the list of APIs here[2].

Here are a few of the more common APIs you may like to use in your plugins:

Dashboard Widgets API—if your plugin adds content (notice information) to the admin dashboard Database API—if you are directly interfacing with the database REST API—lets you make some or all WordPress data (posts, pages, etc.) available to external platforms Options API—if you want your plugin options controlled alongside other admin options Shortcode API—if you plan to make shortcodes a part of your plugin Widgets API—allows your plugin to make configurable widgets available to the theme.

Rule Four: Prefix Your Code

Prefixing your function and class names helps encapsulate your code from other plugins that may also be installed on the same WordPress site. Many plugins interact with the database. If you had a function called save_to_db() and another plugin defines the same function, there is ambiguity. One or both plugins can fail—bringing the entire site to a stand-still.

---

[1] dependant plugin exists: *https://phpa.me/devinvinson-468*
[2] list of APIs here: *https://codex.wordpress.org/WordPress_APIs*

This is an issue within the underlying language of PHP; when it encounters a call to a function with an already used name, it comes to a complete halt and emits a fatal error. For example, if your plugin was named "Plugin Services Manager," prefix your save to database function with psm_. Your function's full name would then be: psm_save_to_db().

This advice goes back to rule two. You could copy well-tested code from a previously developed plugin and therefore be in self-conflict. Although it may not seem efficient to have potentially duplicated code, it is best, in the long run, to be as separated and ensconced as possible with your plugin code. If you find that you use the same functions across plugins, consider making a "base" plugin that your other plugins depend on.

Additionally, you can use PHP's native syntax for namespaces and object-oriented programming to prevent name collisions. Using namespaces prevents naming clashes in large applications by segmenting class and function names. You can read up on namespaces in PHP[3] in the online documentation.

Rule Five: Use OOP Whenever Possible

This advice is a general practice for anything related to PHP code. Object-oriented programming is a better approach to writing and organizing code. It makes your code more reusable and adaptable. It also helps with the separation of coding concerns, as already pointed out above. OOP allows for the encapsulation of code into blueprints called classes, which define how objects of a particular class behave. These blueprints house both properties (variables) and methods (functions) specific to that object. Once instantiated, the object is treated as one item with defined behaviors. For further reading on OOP check out these resources:

- Simplifying WordPress's functions.php with OOP[4]
- Introduction to Object-Oriented PHP for WordPress Developers[5]

Rule Six: Follow Secure Coding Practices

Even in this modern age of software development, we need to reiterate the importance of secure code. Keeping your site safe from malicious actors is an ongoing process, but it can save you time and effort by minimizing the risk that your site is taken over, defaced, or used to steal user data. Here are some general guidelines for writing secure code.

1. Secure and filter input. You should never trust any information coming from an outside/unknown source, especially if your plugin allows for things like public

---

[3]   namespaces in PHP: *https://php.net/language.namespaces.rationale*
[4]   *Simplifying WordPress's functions.php with OOP:* *https://phpa.me/wsmith-wp-oop*
[5]   *Introduction to Object-Oriented PHP for WordPress Developers:* *https://phpa.me/wpshout-oop-course*

comments. If you're expecting a state abbreviation, US phone number, or zip code, validate that the input looks like what you expected.

2. Escape all output. Never display user-submitted data without escaping it first. Doing so prevents cross-site scripting (XSS) attacks where someone tries to add HTML or Javascript code to your page. (Cross-Site Scripting) site attacks.

3. Confirm only authorized users have expected access levels granted to your plugin. Always ensure your site contributors have roles with appropriate levels of access. You should never be in danger of being "hacked" by an authorized user with unnecessary access. There's no need to be hacked by someone who has authorized access to your site. Be sure to give your site contributors appropriate access roles to complete their tasks and no more.

4. Protect database insertions with prepared statements and filtered data. Clean data going into your database is always preferred and prevents frequent attacks. Use prepared statements to avoid SQL injection attacks.

WordPress has several functions that can help secure your code and data; be sure to employ them when and where needed. Look here for details on this security topic[6].

Rule Seven: Minimize Using Sessions If Possible

Sessions should only be used where really needed. WordPress.org recommends that if you must use a session, you at least encapsulate it within a function. Using sessions can conflict with server-based caching features that are often set up on commercial hosting platforms. Using PHP functions like session_start(), ob_start(), and ob_end_flush() can conflict with products like Varnish and NGINX that cache content on a site-wide basis. This can cause the host to not work as expected and may get your plugin banned from the host as a result. It may be a non-issue issue if you are running your hosting platform, but the nature of plugin creation is to allow the masses to use them, so it is better not to use code caching methods.

Rule Eight: Use WordPress Functions Instead Of PHP Functions

Rule eight is a similar point to the one above about APIs. WordPress has many functions that mimic or improve upon native PHP functions. There are often specific situations within WordPress that the native PHP function does not account for. The WordPress replacement function takes these kinds of issues into account. Therefore, your code benefits from these improvements if you use the WordPress equivalent. One example of this is the augmentation of PHP's strip_tags() function into WordPress' wp_strip_all_tags()[7] function. Read the latter's documentation for an example.

---

[6] security topic: https://phpa.me/wpdev-plugins-security
[7] wp_strip_all_tags(): https://phpa.me/wpdev-wp-strip-all-tags

Rule Nine: Always Use The WordPress Database API

WordPress has its database class accessed through $wpdb; use it and its methods at all times. Also, use prepared statements when building your SQL commands to avoid making your code vulnerable to SQL injections. See the $wpdb class documentation here[8] for usage details.

Further Guidelines

That covers the best practices of plugin creation, in general, and at a high level. Be sure to review all of the guidelines[9] for plugin development.

> NOTE: Your development platform should be separate from any live WordPress installations while building your plugins. Some major development projects even have another platform, often called a staging site to perform testing.

Example Plugin

Let's carry on with building an example plugin over the course of this chapter following the best practice guidelines as we progress. First, let's discuss what this plugin will do. It will be basic in its functionality and features. We also want to show how to interact with the front and backend of WordPress—the public and admin areas, respectively. We review processes like connecting to the database, plugin installation, activation, and removal of the plugin. With these basic concepts and integration points, you can get started and create useful plugins for the WordPress world.

Our plugin allows a website visitor to provide their name and email address on a sidebar-based form. Upon opt-in confirmation, we store any collected email addresses in the database in our own table. We can use the contact information to announce when we publish new blog posts on the website. The admin pages allow for turning on or off this new post announcement process and manual data entry. The plugin can also list all the collected data and delete selected emails from the admin area. The email owner can unsubscribe at any time via a link embedded in the emails that they receive via the plugin. We're keeping this a simple example plugin, as previously mentioned. Therefore, we are not creating any shortcode compatibility or adding extra feature add-ons like editing content on the admin side. This code will be free to use and to extend.

---

[8] here: https://phpa.me/wpdev-wpdb
[9] guidelines: https://phpa.me/wpdev-plugin-practices

Basic Files And Folder Layouts

Let's get started with the basic folder structure of a typical WordPress plugin; see Figure 5.1 as a structural example.

The code should be in its own folder under the wp-content/plugins folder (3). If your plugin name is multi-worded, use hyphens between the words and keep the folder name all lowercase to avoid any potential operating system issues. Our plugin will be called architect-subscribers. You should try to name the plugin as descriptively as possible to give users an idea of who created the plugin and what it is meant to do. The primary plugin file name should be the same as the folder name but with a .php extension (architect-subscribers.php). Regardless of whether you plan to make your plugin commercially available, it's always a good idea to have a readme.txt file accompanying the plugin to explain what it is, any dependencies required, and configuration notes in more detail. Read here for some guidelines on the content of the readme.txt file[10].

Figure 5.1.

Plugin folder structure is flexible but should include the following folders at the very least.

- assets—screenshots of your plugin
- css—where your CSS (cascading style sheets) are stored
- images—where your plugin images and icons are stored
- includes—where your plugin code files go
- js—where any JavaScript or jQuery code is stored

---

[10] readme.txt file: https://phpa.me/wp-readme-works

Next, we build the code for the main PHP plugin file. This file sets up most of the plugin's environment and establishes the main menu on the admin side. However, before we build the menu structure, we need to register the plugin within the WordPress ecosystem. To do this, we include the plugin metadata at the beginning of the main file, which names the plugin, gives the contact references, and establishes the license under which the plugin code is released to the public. Listing 5.1 shows the commented code block, which determines all of this information.

Listing 5.1.

```php
1. <?php
2. /*
3.   Plugin Name: Architect Subscribers
4.   Plugin URI:  https://paladin-bs.com/plugins/
5.   Description: Plugin sample for teaching plugin Development.
6.   Author:  Peter MacIntyre
7.   Version: 1.2
8.   Author URI:  https://paladin-bs.com/peter-macintyre/
9.   Details URI: https://paladin-bs.com
10.  License: GPL2
11.  License URI: https://www.gnu.org/licenses/gpl-2.0.html
12.
13.  Architect Subscribers is free software: you can redistribute it and/or modify
14.  it under the terms of the GNU General Public License as published by
15.  the Free Software Foundation, either version 2 of the License, or
16.  any later version.
17.
18.  Architect Subscribers is distributed in the hope that it will be useful,
19.  but WITHOUT ANY WARRANTY; without even the implied warranty of
20.  MERCHANTABILITY or FITNESS FOR A PARTICULAR PURPOSE. See the
21.  GNU General Public License for more details.
22.
23.  See License URI for full details.
24. */
```

Here we give the plugin its name, its description, its version number and author, its URI for where it can be found, and its license. Generally, the license is the GPL2 license; we also provide the URI for where this license can be further explored. Having this block of comments at the beginning of the file registers the plugin on the list of installed (active or inactive) plugins within the WordPress admin area. If you fail to format these settings properly, you risk not having the plugin display on this list. Formatting accuracy is essential. Figure 5.2 shows the results of proper formatting by listing the plugin on the plugins page.

Following the plugin description comment block, we start writing the code that sets up defined constants for path and file location used throughout the plugin. It's best to set these up at the outset of your plugin code, so they can be used anywhere and can be easily located if we need to make changes in future versions. You might want to have these directives in an include file to have them all in a separate manageable location. We'll use these constants frequently in our code. Having them available as constants removes expensive function calls and keeps our code readable (Listing 5.2).

Figure 5.2.

Listing 5.2.

```php
1.  <?php
2.  if (!defined('ARCHITECT_PLUGIN_URL')) {
3.      define('ARCHITECT_PLUGIN_URL', plugin_dir_url(__FILE__));
4.  }
5.
6.  if (!defined('ARCHITECT_ICON')) {
7.      define('ARCHITECT_ICON', ARCHITECT_PLUGIN_URL . 'images/logo_only_orange.png');
8.  }
9.
10. if (!defined('ARCHITECT_LOGO')) {
11.     define('ARCHITECT_LOGO', ARCHITECT_PLUGIN_URL . 'images/logo_orange.png');
12. }
13.
14. // for proper .php file inclusion
15. if (!defined('ARCHITECT_PLUGIN_FILENAME')) {
16. // looks like: /var/www/wordpress/plugins/wp-content/plugins/architect-plugin/architect-plugin.php
17.     define('ARCHITECT_PLUGIN_FILENAME', __FILE__);
18. }
19.
20. if (!defined('ARCHITECT_PLUGIN_FILEPATH')) {
21. //  looks like: /var/www/wordpress/plugins/wp-content/plugins/architect-plugin
22.     define('ARCHITECT_PLUGIN_FILEPATH', dirname(ARCHITECT_PLUGIN_FILENAME));
23. }
24.
25. if (!defined('ARCHITECT_PLUGIN_FILEPATH_INCLUDES')) {
26. //  looks like: /var/www/wordpress/plugins/wp-content/plugins/architect-plugin/includes/
27.     define('ARCHITECT_PLUGIN_FILEPATH_INCLUDES',
28.         dirname(ARCHITECT_PLUGIN_FILENAME) . "/includes/");
29. }
```

Here we are combining a PHP function, `define()`[11] with a WordPress function `plugin_dir_url()`[12] to get what we want. We define constants that return plugin paths with URL references (`https://...`) and some with direct file path access (`/home2/paladip9/public_html/plugins/wp-content...`). This helps us reference plugin supporting files and images as we need them. The paths with the URL references allow for including resources like images or media files on a web page shown to users. In contrast, the direct path allows for including other code files, as needed by the plugin.

To that point, we want to bring in two resources to our plugin from the outset: a CSS file and a JavaScript file. The following code (Listing 5.3) accomplishes this task.

Listing 5.3.

```
1. function architect_js_add_script()
2. {
3.     $js_path = ARCHITECT_PLUGIN_URL . 'js/architect-scripts.js';
4.     wp_enqueue_script('architect-js', $js_path);
5. }
6.
7. add_action('init', 'architect_js_add_script');
8.
9. function architect_css_add_script()
10. {
11.     wp_register_style('architect_custom_admin_css',
12.         ARCHITECT_PLUGIN_URL . 'css/architect-custom.css',
13.         false, '1.0.0');
14.     wp_enqueue_style('architect_custom_admin_css');
15. }
16.
17. add_action('admin_print_styles', 'architect_css_add_script');
```

The JavaScript file is loaded with the `wp_enqueue_script()`[13] WordPress function and triggered with the `add_action()`[14] function, which tells WordPress when to make it available. We are also making use of our previously defined constants for building the path to where the files are located. We use the "init" option to make sure the JavaScript is linked when WordPress is initially loaded.

We follow a similar approach with the CSS code, except we use the "admin_print_styles" trigger to only bring in the CSS code when rendering an admin page. We want the CSS loaded only on WordPress's admin side, as we don't need to make use of it on the public side

---

[11] define(): *https://php.net/define*
[12] plugin_dir_url(): *https://phpa.me/wpdev-plugin-dir-url*
[13] wp_enqueue_script(): *https://phpa.me/wp-enque-script*
[14] add_action(): *https://phpa.me/wp-add-action*

of our plugin. These add_action() options—also called hooks—are many and varied and can be reviewed at Plugin API and Action Reference[15].

These files are all included in the plugin package listing accompanying this book.

Collecting And Saving Data

We cover this topic with one example, as several locations within the plugin receive data and save it to the database. This serves as an example and a template for all of them. First, we need to reiterate the point that we need to be diligent in our security, so our examples build prepared statements and sanitize incoming data to prevent SQL injection vulnerabilities. The example we are using is saving data from within the admin portion of the plugin where the administrator can manually collect names and emails. The full code for this is in Listing 5.4.

Listing 5.4.

```php
1.  <?php
2.
3.  /* ============ */
4.  /* --- MAIN --- */
5.  /* ============ */
6.  if (isset($_POST['submit'])) {
7.      check_form();
8.  } else {
9.      $message = "Provide the data for the new subscriber";
10.     show_form($message);
11. }
12.
13. /* ======== */
14. /* show_form */
15. /* ======== */
16. function show_form($message, $label = "", $type = "OK")
17. { ?>
18.     <div class="wrap">
19.         <img id='page_title_img' title="Architect Sample Plugin"
20.             src="<?= ARCHITECT_LOGO; ?>">
21.         <h1 id='page_title'><?= esc_html(get_admin_page_title()); ?></h1>
22.
23.         <form action="" method="post">
24.             <table class="TableOverride">
25.                 <tr class="TableOverride">
26.                     <td colspan="2" align="center">
27.                         <?php arch_custom_admin_notice($message, $type); ?>
```

[15] Plugin API and Action Reference: https://phpa.me/codex-action-ref

```
28.                         </td>
29.                     </tr>
30.                     <tr class="TableOverride">
31.                         <td class="left_col">
32.                             <p style='display: inline; <?php if ($label == "full_name") {
33.                                 echo "color:red";
34.                             } ?>'>Full Name:</p>
35.                             <p style='color: red; display: inline'>*</p>
36.                         </td>
37.                         <td class="right_col">
38.                             <input type="text" name="full_name"
39.                                     value="<?php if ($print_again) {
40.                                         echo $_POST['full_name'];
41.                                     } ?>">
42.                         </td>
43.                     </tr>
44.                     <tr class="TableOverride">
45.                         <td class="left_col">
46.                             <p style='display: inline; <?php if ($label == "email") {
47.                                 echo "color:red";
48.                             } ?>'>email:</p>
49.                             <p style='color: red; display: inline'>*</p>
50.                         </td>
51.                         <td class="right_col">
52.                             <input type="text" name="email"
53.                                     value="<?php if ($print_again) {
54.                                         echo $_POST['email'];
55.                                     } ?>">
56.                         </td>
57.                     </tr>
58.                     <tr class="TableOverride">
59.                         <td colspan="2" align="center">
60.                             <?php submit_button("Save Settings", "primary", "submit"); ?>
61.                         </td>
62.                     </tr>
63.                 </table>
64.                 <?php wp_nonce_field('nonce_action', 'nonce_field'); ?>
65.             </form>
66.     </div>
67. <?php
68. }
69.
70. /* ========= */
71. /* check_form */
72. /* ========= */
73. function check_form()
74. {
75.     global $wpdb;
76.     $print_again = false;
77.     $label = "";
78.
79.     $full_name = sanitize_text_field($_POST['full_name']);
```

```
80.      $email = sanitize_email($_POST['email']);
81.
82.      /* =============================== */
83.      /* data integrity checks, data massage */
84.      /* =============================== */
85.      if (!isset($_POST['nonce_field']) || !wp_verify_nonce($_POST['nonce_field'], 'nonce_action')) {
86.          $print_again = true;
87.          $message = "<b>Security validation of the nonce failed.</b>";
88.      }
89.      if (empty($email)) {
90.          $print_again = true;
91.          $label = "email";
92.          $return_message = "eMail cannot be blank.";
93.      }
94.      if ($email !== "" && filter_var($email, FILTER_VALIDATE_EMAIL) == false) {
95.          $print_again = true;
96.          $label = "email";
97.          $return_message = "eMail is malformed";
98.      }
99.      if (empty($full_name)) {
100.         $print_again = true;
101.         $label = "full_name";
102.         $return_message = "Full Name cannot be blank.";
103.     }
104.     if (empty($full_name) && empty($email)) {
105.         $print_again = true;
106.         $return_message = "Full Name and eMail cannot both be blank, we need something...";
107.     }
108.     // check to see if we already have the email on file
109.     $result = $wpdb->get_row($wpdb->prepare(
110.             "SELECT `architect_contacts_id`
111.              FROM `architect_contacts` WHERE `email` = %s", $email)
112.     );
113.
114.     if ($result) {
115.         $print_again = true;
116.         $label = "email";
117.         $return_message = "That email is already on file.";
118.     }
119.     /* ======================= */
120.     /* end data integrity checks  */
121.     /* ======================= */
122.
123.     if ($print_again == true) {
124.         $type = "Error";
125.         show_form($return_message, $label, $type);
126.     } else {
127.         /* ======================= */
128.         /* prep for saving the data    */
129.         /* ======================= */
130.         $uniq_token = arch_unique_token();
131.
```

```
132.        // save with name
133.        $wpdb->query($wpdb->prepare("INSERT INTO
134.                `architect_contacts` (`architect_token`, `full_name`, `email`)
135.                VALUES (%s, %s, %s )",
136.            $uniq_token, $full_name, $email)
137.        );
138.
139.        arch_send_welcome_email($email, $uniq_token, $full_name);
140.
141.        $return_message = "Contact Information saved...the new member will still have to opt-in";
142.        show_form($return_message);
143.    }
144. }
145.
146. // display custom admin notice
147. function arch_custom_admin_notice($message, $type)
148. {
149.    switch ($type) {
150.        case "OK":
151.            $class_type = "notice-success is-dismissible";
152.            break;
153.        case "Error":
154.            $class_type = "notice-error is-dismissible";
155.            break;
156.        case "Warning":
157.            $class_type = "notice-warning is-dismissible";
158.            break;
159.        case "Info":
160.            $class_type = "notice-info is-dismissible";
161.            break;
162.    }
163.    $outstring =
164.        "<div class='notice " . $class_type . "'><p> $message </p></div>";
165.    echo $outstring;
166. }
167.
168. add_action('admin_notices', 'arch_custom_admin_notice');
```

The data entry screen looks like that shown in Figure 5.3.

Be sure to review the show_form() function to see how the form is constructed and how the data fields are prepared for accepting data. You can see how we designate required fields and we prepare the field labels for changing their color should there

Figure 5.3.

be an error reported. Besides that, the code of note is located in the check_form() function and is follows:

```
$full_name  = sanitize_text_field($_POST['full_name']) ;
$email = sanitize_email($_POST['email']) ;
```

Here, we use specialized WordPress functions for sanitizing input. There are many specific functions you should use, depending on the kind of data you are accepting. In this case, we are filtering the input for text data and more narrowly email address patterns. For a full list of the specific sanitizing functions, visit this page on securing input[16].

We then perform our data entry validation checks on the entered data. If everything looks acceptable, we prepare the SQL statement within the $wpdb->prepare() function embedded within a $wpdb->query() function. We can perform this easily in two steps, but it's a little more succinct, as we see below.

```
$wpdb->query(
    $wpdb->prepare(
        "INSERT INTO `architect_contacts` (`full_name`, `email`)
         VALUES (%s, %s )",
        $full_name, $email
    )
);
```

Next, we call arch_send_welcome_email() located in our functions include file (Listing 5.4), to send a welcome email. In the content of the email, we ask the email owner to confirm their desire to be on our list, where we use the token prefix to add to the front of the reply URL—double opt-in approach. When the signor confirms their intention by clicking on the link, we pickup that response and make our confirmation field equal to 1. Finally, we prepare the message information that we want to show to the admin user and re-display the form with a call to the show_form() function.

Of note here is that we have to create HTML forms to collect our data from the end-user (or, in this case, the admin user). The form has to be precise in its form fields, and we are using similarly named labels to manage our messaging for error handling. We use a variable called $print_again to control the code's reaction to errors.

---

[16] *securing input:* https://phpa.me/wpdev-securing-input

Listing Collected Data

We want to show the admin user all the collected email addresses in a list format. We can use the `WP_List_Table`[17] class provided by WordPress and adjust it to our needs. Using this class, you also have access to other features that are built-in like pagination of the list, consistent layout of the data, and the ability to sort on any designated column. Listing 5.5 shows our customizations for it.

Listing 5.5.

```php
<?php
if (!class_exists('WP_List_Table')) {
    // in case the class is ever removed from WP Core use this copy
    require_once(ABSPATH . 'wp-content/plugins/architect-plugin/includes/wp_list_class/class-wp-list-table.php');
}

class Architect_List_Table extends WP_List_Table
{
    /* ==== constructor === */
    function __construct()
    {
        global $status, $page;
        parent::__construct([
            'singular' => 'Subscriber',
            //singular name of the listed records
            'plural' => 'Subscribers'
            //plural name of the listed records
        ]);
    }

    function column_default($item, $column_name)
    {
        return $item[$column_name];
    }

    function column_email($item)
    {
        $output =
            "<em><a href='mailto:$item[email]' target='_top'> " . $item['email'] . "</em>";
        return $output;
    }

    function column_email_optin_date($item)
    {
        if ($item['email_optin_date']) {
            $return_string =
                '<em>' . date('M j, Y', strtotime($item['email_optin_date'])) . '</em>';
        } else {
```

[17] `WP_List_Table`: *https://phpa.me/wpdev-wp-list-table*

```
39.        $return_string = "";
40.      }
41.      return $return_string;
42.   }
43.
44.   function column_full_name($item)
45.   {
46.      // $_REQUEST['page'] used so action will be done on curren page in delete a href string
47.      $actions = [
48.         'delete' => sprintf(
49.            '<a href="?page=%s&action=delete&id=%s">%s</a>',
50.            $_REQUEST['page'], $item['architect_contacts_id'], 'Delete'
51.         )
52.      ];
53.      return sprintf('%s %s',
54.         $item['full_name'],
55.         $this->row_actions($actions)
56.      );
57.   }
58.
59.   function column_cb($item)
60.   {
61.      return sprintf(
62.         '<input type="checkbox" name="id[]" value="%s" />',
63.         $item['architect_contacts_id']
64.      );
65.   }
66.
67.   function get_columns()
68.   {
69.      $columns = [
70.         'cb' => '<input type="checkbox" />',
71.         //Render a checkbox instead of text
72.         'full_name' => 'Subscriber Name',
73.         'email' => 'EMail Address',
74.         'email_optin_date' => 'EMail Opt-in Date'
75.      ];
76.      return $columns;
77.   }
78.
79.   function get_sortable_columns()
80.   {
81.      $sortable_columns = [
82.         'full_name' => ['full_name', true],
83.         //true means it's already sorted
84.         'email' => ['email', false],
85.         'email_optin_date' => ['email_optin_date', false]
86.      ];
87.      return $sortable_columns;
88.   }
89.
```

```
90.    function get_bulk_actions()
91.    {
92.       $actions = [
93.          'delete' => 'Delete'
94.       ];
95.       return $actions;
96.    }
97.
98.    function process_bulk_action()
99.    {
100.      global $wpdb;
101.      $table_name = 'architect_contacts';
102.      if ('delete' === $this->current_action()) {
103.         $ids = isset($_REQUEST['id']) ? $_REQUEST['id'] : [];
104.         if (is_array($ids)) {
105.            $ids = implode(',', $ids);
106.         }
107.         if (!empty($ids)) {
108.            $wpdb->query("DELETE FROM $table_name WHERE architect_contacts_id IN($ids)");
109.         }
110.      }
111.   }
112.
113.   function prepare_items($search = null)
114.   {
115.      global $wpdb;
116.      $table_name = 'architect_contacts';
117.      $per_page =
118.         10; // constant, how much records will be shown per page
119.      $columns = $this->get_columns();
120.      $hidden = [];
121.      $sortable = $this->get_sortable_columns();
122.      // here we configure table headers, defined in our methods
123.      $this->_column_headers = [$columns, $hidden, $sortable];
124.      // [OPTIONAL] process bulk action if any
125.      $this->process_bulk_action();
126.      // will be used in pagination settings
127.      $total_items = $wpdb->get_var(
128.         "SELECT COUNT(`architect_contacts_id`) FROM `$table_name`"
129.      );
130.      // prepare query params, as usual current page, order by and order direction
131.      $paged = isset($_REQUEST['paged']) ?
132.         max(0, intval($_REQUEST['paged']) - 1) : 0;
133.
134.      $allowed_keys = array_keys($this->get_sortable_columns());
135.
136.      $orderby = 'full_name'; // defaule
137.      if (isset($_REQUEST['orderby']) && in_array($_REQUEST['orderby'], $allowed_keys)) {
138.         $orderby = $_REQUEST['orderby'];
139.      }
140.
```

```
141.        $order = 'asc'; // default
142.        if (isset($_REQUEST['order']) && in_array($_REQUEST['order'], ['asc', 'desc'])) {
143.            $order = $_REQUEST['order'];
144.        }
145.
146.        /* If the value is not NULL, do a search for it. */
147.        if ($search != null) {
148.
149.            // Trim and sanitize Search Term
150.            $search = trim($search);
151.
152.            /* Notice how you can search multiple columns for your search term easily, and return one data set */
153.            $sql = $wpdb->prepare(
154.              "SELECT * FROM $table_name
155.                    WHERE `full_name` LIKE '%%s%%' OR `email` LIKE '%%s%%'
156.                    ORDER BY $orderby $order LIMIT %d OFFSET %d",
157.                $search, $search, $per_page, $paged
158.            );
159.            $this->items = $wpdb->get_results($sql, ARRAY_A);
160.        } else {
161.            $this->items = $wpdb->get_results($wpdb->prepare(
162.              "SELECT * FROM $table_name
163.                    ORDER BY $orderby $order
164.                    LIMIT %d OFFSET %d", $per_page, $paged
165.            ), ARRAY_A);
166.        }
167.
168.        // [REQUIRED] configure pagination
169.        $this->set_pagination_args([
170.            'total_items' => $total_items, // total items defined above
171.            'per_page' => $per_page,
172.            // per page constant defined at top of method
173.            'total_pages' => ceil($total_items / $per_page)
174.            // calculate pages count
175.        ]);
176.    }
177.
178. } //class
```

Listing 5.6 shows how to use the class in your plugin code.

Listing 5.6.

```
1. <?php
2.
3. $myListTable = new architect_List_Table();
4.
5. if (isset($_REQUEST['s'])) {
6.     $myListTable->prepare_items($_REQUEST['s']);
7. } else {
```

```php
 8.     $myListTable->prepare_items();
 9. }
10.
11. $current_action = $myListTable->current_action();
12.
13. /* ========================= */
14. /* == display page header ======= */
15. /* ========================= */
16. ?>
17.     <div class="wrap">
18.         <img id='page_title_img' title="Architect Sample Plugin"
19.             src="<?= ARCHITECT_LOGO; ?>">
20.         <h1 id='page_title'><?= esc_html(get_admin_page_title()); ?></h1>
21.
22.         <div style="background:#ECECEC;border:1px solid #CCC;padding:0 10px;margin-
    top:5px;border-radius:5px;-moz-border-radius:5px;-webkit-border-radius:5px;">
23.             <p>Manage your subscriber information here</p>
24.         </div>
25.     </div>
26. <?php
27.
28. if ($current_action === 'delete') {
29.     $message = '<div class="updated below-h2" id="message"><p>'
30.             . sprintf('Items deleted: %d', count($_REQUEST['id'])) . '</p></div>';
31. }
32.
33. if ($current_action === 'edit') {
34.     // bring in the edit form
35.     $edit_path =
36.         ARCHITECT_PLUGIN_INCLUDES . 'architect-edit-subscribers.inc';
37.     require_once($edit_path);
38. } else {
39.     ?>
40.     <h2><?php echo 'Subscribers'; ?></h2>
41.     <?= $message; ?>
42.     <!-- Forms are NOT created automatically, so you need to wrap the table in one to use
    features like bulk actions -->
43.     <form method="get">
44.         <!-- For plugins, we also need to ensure that the form posts back to our current
    page -->
45.         <input type="hidden" name="page"
46.             value="<?= $_REQUEST['page'] ?>"/>
47.     <?php $myListTable->search_box('Search', 'search_id'); ?>
48.         <!-- Now we can render the completed list table -->
49.         <?php $myListTable->display() ?>
50.     </form>
51. <?php } ?>
```

The code in the main plugin file architect-subscribers.php that creates the listing page upon the menu click is thus:

```
function architect_list_subscribers() {
    // check user capabilities
    if (!current_user_can('manage_options')) {
        return;
    }

    require_once(ARCHITECT_PLUGIN_FILEPATH_INCLUDES . "architect-list-subscribers.php");
}
```

Here we are testing again to see if the user has permission to access the page and if that passes muster, we load the code with a require_once() PHP call.

The page, when loaded, looks like Figure 5.4

Figure 5.4.

Admin Menu Creation

We can use several functions to customize the menu system inside the WordPress administration area, depending on what menu area you want to change. Here is a list of those functions and where they have an impact. To affect sub-menus, you can use any of these functions[18].

Function	Description
add_menu_page()	Add a menu item at the top level of the admin menu[19].
add_dashboard_page()	Add a submenu page to the Dashboard menu.
add_posts_page()	Add a submenu page to the Posts menu.
add_media_page()	Add a submenu page to the Media menu.
add_pages_page()	Add a submenu page to the Pages menu.
add_comments_page()	Add a submenu page to the Comments menu.
add_theme_page()	Add a submenu page to the Appearance menu.
add_plugins_page()	Add a submenu page to the Plugins menu.
add_users_page()	Add a submenu page to the Users menu.
add_management_page()	Add a submenu page to the Tools menu.
add_options_page()	Add a submenu page to the Settings menu.

[18] these functions: https://phpa.me/wpdev-sub-menus
[19] admin menu: https://phpa.me/wpdev-top-menus

Since we are creating our own top-level menu and submenu system we use the add_menu_page( ) function along with its "cousin" add_submenu_page( ) function to tie the submenu items to our top-level parent. We need a settings page for our plugin on the admin menu, a page for manually adding email contacts, and a page listing the existing email addresses we have collected. The code to build this menu structure is made almost entirely of Word-Press functions since we are adjusting the

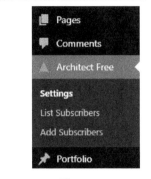

Figure 5.5.

administration area of WordPress. We, therefore, want a menu that looks like the one shown in Figure 5.5.

The code for this menu structure resides in the main plugin file, in our case architect-subscribers.php, in the architecht_menu( ) function, and looks like Listing 5.7

Listing 5.7.

```
1.  function architect_menu()
2.  {
3.      add_menu_page(
4.          'Architect Free: Architect Settings',    // Page & tab title
5.          'Architect Free',    // Menu title
6.          'manage_options',    // Capability option
7.          'architect_Admin',    // Menu slug
8.          'architect_config_page',// menu destination function call
9.          ARCHITECT_ICON, // menu icon path defined earlier
10.         25 // menu position level
11.     );
12.     add_submenu_page(
13.         'architect_Admin',// parent slug
14.         'Architect Free: Configurations Page', // page title
15.         'Settings',// menu title - can be different than parent
16.         'manage_options',  // options
17.         'architect_Admin'
18.     ); // menu slug to match top level (go to the same link)
19.     add_submenu_page(
20.         'architect_Admin',    // parent menu slug
21.         'Architect Free: Manage Subscribers', // page title
```

```
22.         'List Subscribers',// menu title
23.         'manage_options',  // capability
24.         'architect_list_subs',   // menu slug
25.         'architect_list_subscribers' // callable function
26.     );
27.     add_submenu_page(
28.         'architect_Admin',// parent menu slug
29.         'Architect Free: Add a New Subscriber', // page title
30.         'Add Subscribers',  // menu title
31.         'manage_options',   // capability
32.         'architect_add_subs', // menu slug
33.         'architect_add_subscribers'  // callable function
34.     );
35. }
36.
37. // call add action func to build the menu
38. add_action('admin_menu', 'architect_menu');
```

This code builds the menu we want. You can see we are using the previously defined constant of ARCHITECT_ICON, which points to the file location of our plugin's custom menu icon (the orange A) seen in Figure 5.5.

Note that the menu position option on the add_menu_page function (value of 25) is an arbitrary number that can only be used as an approximation. There is no way to tell where position 25, in this case, would land within any given WordPress installation. Therefore, it is used to provide an approximate location of where you would like the menu to appear. Also, note that the first two menu item functions refer to the "architect_Admin" menu slug. This makes our plugin's main menu item call the same settings page as the first submenu item so you can go directly to the settings menu without expanding the submenu options first.

The last thing to note in this code segment is the add_action() call, which creates the menu with the hook call of "admin_menu". It calls the architect_menu() function, which encompasses all the menu building code. Each submenu item then calls its function (defined later in the code) to load their respective pages within the WordPress admin area for the plugin's use. The first page to be accessible on the menu then is the plugins settings page; let's look into how this is created.

Admin Page Development

If you look at the code above that creates the menu for our plugin, you see the callable function defined is architect_config_page(). This tells WordPress to call a function by this name when either the plugin's main menu or the settings submenu is clicked. The code for this function follows:

```
function architect_config_page() {
    // check user capabilities
    if (!current_user_can('manage_options')) {
        return;
    }

    require_once(ARCHITECT_PLUGIN_FILEPATH_INCLUDES . "architect-config-page.php");
}
```

Here we can see it is two lines of code. First, we need to test whether the currently logged in user has permission to execute this menu item. We are checking to see if the user has the manage_options permission level, and if not, then we return and leave this process. If the logged-in user does not have the appropriate level of access (editor level, for example), the plugin does not continue, and its menu item does not appear to the user. The logged-in user without the appropriate access can not see the plugin menu items and, therefore, may not be aware the plugin exists.

WordPress has a litany of permission levels, and they can all be viewed here[20]. manage_options is an administrator-level access which allows for the creation of custom top-level menu items as well as the ability to add menu items to the settings menu section. This ensures the logged-in user has admin-level access with at least permissions to see alterations to the settings menu where some plugins set their access points. If you want to alter the level of permission required to run your plugin, you should check out the list of admin-level access points and choose appropriately.

Once that check passes, we again employ a defined constant pointing to the folder where we store all of our included code files and bring in the architect-config-page.php code file, which generates the plugin's settings page form.

Form Management

Our admin settings page is quite simple and, therefore, we don't need to discuss much code here. We call two functions from the same code file, depending on whether the form was submitted. We have a controlling if block at the top of the file, which determines the

---

[20] *viewed here:* <u>*https://phpa.me/wordpress-roles*</u>

submitted state; it calls show_form() or check_form() appropriately. For added form security, we have added a call to the wp_nonce_field()[21] function, which helps verify the submission of the form data originated from the same client. We verify this code in the check_form() function by testing for the nonce information in the $_POST array. The settings form looks like the one shown in Figure 5.6.

The full code for this settings page is in Listing 5.8. The highlights here are that we recall the same file for showing and checking the submitted data depending on the state of the submit button and calling

Figure 5.6.

the appropriate function to show or check the form. On the display of the form, we have a custom-built function called arch_build_help(), which shows context-sensitive help in a blue circled question mark. The help is stored in the database, and we can easily extend it if we add more fields to the form.

Listing 5.8.

```php
1.  <?php
2.  /* ============ */
3.  /* --- MAIN --- */
4.  /* ============ */
5.  if (isset($_POST['submit'])) {
6.      check_form();
7.  } else {
8.      $message = "Adjust settings to your preferences";
9.      show_form($message);
10. }
11.
12. /* ========= */
13. /* show_form */
14. /* ========= */
15. function show_form($message, $label = "", $type = "OK")
16. {
17.     global $print_again, $wpdb; ?>
18.       <div class="wrap">
19.         <img id='page_title_img' title="Architect Sample Plugin"
20.             src="<?= ARCHITECT_LOGO; ?>">
21.         <h1 id='page_title'><?php esc_html(get_admin_page_title()); ?></h1>
22.
```

---

[21] wp_nonce_field(): *https://phpa.me/wpdev-using-nonces*

```
23.        <form action="" method="post">
24.            <table class="TableOverride form-table">
25.                <tr class="TableOverride">
26.                    <td colspan="2" align="center">
27.                        <?php
28.                        arch_custom_admin_notice($message, $type);
29.
30.                        $architect_result =
31.                            $wpdb->get_row($wpdb->prepare("SELECT * FROM `architect_control`
32.        WHERE `architect_control_id` = %d", 1)
33.                            );
34.                        ?></td>
35.                </tr>
36.                <tr class="TableOverride">
37.                    <td class="left_col">
38.                        <p style='display: inline; <?php if ($label == "email_updates") {
39.                            echo "color:red";
40.                        } ?>'>Send Post Updates by eMail?</p>
41.                    </td>
42.                    <td class="right_col"><input type="checkbox"
43.                                            name="email_updates" <?php
44.                    if ($print_again) {
45.                        echo $_POST['email_updates'] == "on" ?
46.                            "CHECKED" : "";
47.                    } else {
48.                        echo $architect_result->email_updates == 1 ?
49.                            "CHECKED" : "";
50.                    }
51.                    ?>></td>
52.                </tr>
53.
54.                <tr class="TableOverride form-field form-required">
55.                    <td class="left_col">
56.                        <p style='display: inline; <?php if ($label == "token_prefix") {
57.                            echo "color:red";
58.                        } ?>'>Token Prefix:(required)</p>
59.
60.                        <?php echo arch_build_help("token_prefix"); ?>
61.
62.                    </td>
63.                    <td class="right_col"><input type="text"
64.                                            name="token_prefix"
65.                                            style="width: 25%;"
66.                                            value="<?php
67.                                            if ($print_again) {
68.                                                echo $_POST['token_prefix'];
69.                                            } else {
70.                                                if ($architect_result->token_prefix) {
71.                                                    echo $architect_result->token_prefix;
72.                                                }
73.                                            }
74.                                            ?>"></td>
75.                </tr>
```

```
76.            <tr class="TableOverride">
77.                <td class="left_col">
78.                    <p style='display: inline; <?php if ($label == "recaptcha_site") {
79.                        echo "color:red";
80.                    } ?>'>Google ReCaptcha Site Key:</p>
81.                    <p style='color: red; display: inline'>*</p>
82.                </td>
83.                <td class="right_col"><input type="password"
84.                                    name="recaptcha_site"
85.                                    id="myGRCSite"
86.                                    value="<?php
87.                                    if ($print_again) {
88.                                        echo sanitize_text_field($_POST['recaptcha_site']);
89.                                    } else {
90.                                        if ($architect_result->grc_site_key) {
91.                                            echo $architect_result->grc_site_key;
92.                                        }
93.                                    }
94.                                    ?>">
95.                </td>
96.            </tr>
97.            <tr class="TableOverride">
98.                <td class="left_col">
99.                    <p style='display: inline; <?php if ($label == "recaptcha_secret") {
100.                        echo "color:red";
101.                    } ?>'>Google ReCaptcha Secret Key:</p>
102.                    <p style='color: red; display: inline'>*</p>
103.                </td>
104.                <td class="right_col"><input type="password"
105.                                    name="recaptcha_secret"
106.                                    id="myGRCSecret"
107.                                    value="<?php
108.                                    if ($print_again) {
109.                                        echo sanitize_text_field($_POST['recaptcha_secret']);
110.                                    } else {
111.                                        if ($architect_result->grc_secret_key) {
112.                                            echo $architect_result->grc_secret_key;
113.                                        }
114.                                    }
115.                                    ?>">
116.                </td>
117.            </tr>
118.            <tr class="TableOverride">
119.                <td> </td>
120.                <td class="right_col">
121.                    <div style="margin-top: 5px; width: 93%; border: 1px solid #004F6D; padding: 5px;
      background: #DAF0F8;">
122.                        You need to register your site with Google
123.                        ReCaptcha. Be sure to set up using the
124.                        ReCaptcha Version 2 checkbox option.
125.                        To do that go here:</br> [<a
126.                            href="https://developers.google.com/recaptcha/"
127.                            target="_blank">Google ReCaptcha
```

```
128.                            Version 2 Checkbox</a>]
129.                        </div>
130.                    </td>
131.                </tr>
132.                <tr class="TableOverride">
133.                    <td colspan="2">
134.                        <?php submit_button("Save Settings", "primary", "submit"); ?>
135.                    </td>
136.                </tr>
137.            </table>
138.            <?php wp_nonce_field('nonce_action', 'nonce_field'); ?>
139.        </form>
140.    </div>
141.    <?php
142. }
143.
144. /* ========== */
145. /* check_form */
146. /* ========== */
147. function check_form()
148. {
149.
150.    global $print_again, $wpdb;
151.
152.    $label = "";
153.    $message = "";
154.    $token_prefix = sanitize_text_field($_POST['token_prefix']);
155.
156.    $GRCSite = $_POST["recaptcha_site"];
157.    $GRCSecret = $_POST["recaptcha_secret"];
158.
159.    /* data integrity checks */
160.
161.    if (!isset($_POST['nonce_field']) || !wp_verify_nonce($_POST['nonce_field'], 'nonce_action')) {
162.        $print_again = true;
163.        $message = "<b>Security validation of the nonce failed.</b>";
164.    }
165.
166.    if (empty($token_prefix)) {
167.        $print_again = true;
168.        $label = "token_prefix";
169.        $message = "<b>token prefix field cannot be blank.</b>";
170.    }
171.    if (empty($GRCSite)) {
172.        $print_again = true;
173.        $label = "recaptcha_site";
174.        $message = "Google ReCaptcha Site Key cannot be blank.";
175.    }
176.    if (empty($GRCSecret)) {
177.        $print_again = true;
178.        $label = "recaptcha_secret";
179.        $message = "Google ReCaptcha Secret Key cannot be blank.";
180.    }
```

```
181.
182.    // end data integrity checking
183.
184.    if ($print_again == true) {
185.        $type = "Error";
186.        show_form($message, $label, $type);
187.    } else {
188.
189.        if ($_POST['email_updates'] == "on") {
190.            $email_updates = 1;
191.        } else {
192.            $email_updates = 0;
193.        }
194.
195.        $config_sql = $wpdb->prepare("UPDATE `architect_control` SET
196.            `email_updates` = %d, `token_prefix` = %s, `grc_site_key` = %s, `grc_secret_key` = %s
197.            WHERE `architect_control_id` = %d",
198.        $email_updates, $token_prefix, $GRCSite, $GRCSecret, 1);
199.
200.        $wpdb->query($config_sql);
201.
202.        $message = "Configuration Changes have been saved";
203.        show_form($message);
204.    }
205. }
206.
207. // display custom admin notice
208. function arch_custom_admin_notice($message, $type)
209. {
210.    switch ($type) {
211.        case "OK":
212.            $class_type = "notice-success is-dismissible";
213.            break;
214.        case "Error":
215.            $class_type = "notice-error is-dismissible";
216.            break;
217.        case "Warning":
218.            $class_type = "notice-warning is-dismissible";
219.            break;
220.        case "Info":
221.            $class_type = "notice-info is-dismissible";
222.            break;
223.    }
224.    $outstring =
225.        "<div class='notice " . $class_type . "'><p> $message </p></div>";
226.    echo $outstring;
227. }
228.
229. add_action('admin_notices', 'arch_custom_admin_notice');
```

In the check_form() function, we verify the data as entered based on validation checks we desire after sanitizing our incoming information. Then, if all is acceptable, we build our SQL prepared statement and call $wbdb->query() on the SQL string to save the submitted form data.

Most plugin forms can be built to follow this pattern with the display and validation checks in the same code file. Also, note that since we called in the CSS code with wp_enqueue_style in the main plugin file, we can reference the CSS in the HTML output generated by the included settings file. As a result, you can see class names used on the HTML table tags like class= "TableOverride".

Creating A Widget

The next area we want to look at is the creation of a plugin widget. Widgets allow site builders to add interactive blocks to defined spots on the WordPress site without any coding. We want to show our form for signing up to our mailing list on the sidebar of our public-facing website, so it is visible on all pages that also display a sidebar—primarily blog pages. A widget is implemented in the widget area of the WordPress admin under the Appearance menu (1). It's displayed and used on the frontend of the site in webpage sidebars. The widget design area shows our named widget, as shown in Figure 5.7.

Figure 5.7.

The implementation of this form on the frontend looks like Figure 5.8.

The code to build this widget is relatively long, shown as Listing 5.9.

Figure 5.8.

Listing 5.9.

```php
1. <?php
2.
3. class arch_contacts_widget extends WP_Widget
4. {
5.     // instantiate the class
6.     function __construct()
7.     {
8.         $widget_ops = [
9.             'classname' => 'architect_contacts_widget_class',
10.            'description' => 'Collect contact information When signing up for new Post Notifications.'
11.        ];
12.        $this->WP_Widget(
13.            'architect_contacts_widget',
14.            'Architect Contacts Widget', // display text on widgets page
15.            $widget_ops);
16.
17.        wp_register_style('arch_custom_widget_css', ARCHITECT_PLUGIN_URL . 'css/arch-widget.css');
18.        wp_enqueue_style('arch_custom_widget_css');
19.    }
20.
21.    // build the widget settings form
22.    function form($instance)
23.    {
24.        $defaults = ['title' => 'News Feed Sign Up'];
25.        $instance = wp_parse_args((array)$instance, $defaults);
26.        $title = $instance['title']; ?>
27.         <p>Title: <input type="text" class="widefat"
28.                        name="<?php echo $this->get_field_name('title'); ?>"
29.                        value="<?php echo esc_attr($title); ?>"/></p>
30.    <?php }
31.
32.    // save widget settings function on admin widget
33.    function update($new_instance, $old_instance)
34.    {
35.        $instance = $old_instance;
36.        $instance['title'] = strip_tags($new_instance['title']);
37.        return $instance;
38.    }
39.
40.    // display the widget
41.    function widget($args, $instance)
42.    {
43.        extract($args);
44.        echo $before_widget;
45.        $title = apply_filters('widget_title', $instance['title']);
46.        if (!empty($title)) {
47.            echo $before_title . $title . $after_title;
48.        };
49.        arch_build_recaptcha_top();
50.        ?>
```

```
51.        <form action="" method="post">
52.
53.            <p> Full Name: <input type="text" class="widefat"
54.                              name="full_name" value=""/></p>
55.
56.            <p> eMail: <input type="text" class="widefat" name="email"
57.                           value=""/></p>
58.
59.          <?php arch_build_recaptcha_main(); ?>
60.          </br>
61.          <input type="submit" name="submit" class="submit_btn"
62.                  value="Join List">
63.
64.          <?php wp_nonce_field('nonce_action', 'nonce_field');
65.
66.          // check that the form was submitted
67.          if (isset($_POST['submit']) && $_POST['submit'] == "Join List") {
68.              echo $this->public_save($_POST);
69.          } ?>
70.        </form>
71.      <?php echo $after_widget;
72.    }
73.    /* ===================== */
74.    /* save public form data */
75.    /* ===================== */
76.    function public_save($FormData)
77.    {
78.        global $wpdb;
79.        $contacts_widget_return_message = "";
80.
81.        $full_name = sanitize_text_field($FormData['full_name']);
82.        $email = sanitize_email($FormData['email']);
83.
84.        /* ==================================== */
85.        /* data integrity checks, data massage */
86.        /* ==================================== */
87.        if (!isset($_POST['nonce_field']) || !wp_verify_nonce($_POST['nonce_field'], 'nonce_action')) {
88.            $print_again = true;
89.            $message = "<b>Security validation of the nonce failed.</b>";
90.        }
91.
92.        if ($email == "") {
93.            $print_again = true;
94.            $label = "email";
95.            $contacts_widget_return_message = "eMail cannot be blank.";
96.        }
97.        if ($email !== "" && filter_var($email, FILTER_VALIDATE_EMAIL) == false) {
98.            $print_again = true;
99.            $label = "email";
100.           $contacts_widget_return_message = "eMail is malformed";
101.       }
```

```
102.      if ($full_name == "") {
103.          $print_again = true;
104.          $label = "full_name";
105.          $contacts_widget_return_message =
106.              "Full Name cannot be blank.";
107.      }
108.      /* ========================= */
109.      /* end data integrity checks */
110.      /* ========================= */
111.      if (!$print_again) {
112.
113.          /* ======================= */
114.          /* prep for saving the data */
115.          /* ======================= */
116.
117.          // if only given an email, check to see if we already have it
118.          if ($email != "") {
119.              $result = $wpdb->get_row($wpdb->prepare("SELECT `architect_contacts_id`
120.                      FROM `architect_contacts`
121.                      WHERE `email` = %s",
122.                  $email)
123.              );
124.              if ($result->architect_contacts_id) {
125.                  $contacts_widget_return_message =
126.                      "<p class='error_message'>That email is already on file.<br/>Thanks for previously
    joining us!</p>";
127.              } else {
128.                  // save with name
129.                  $wpdb->query($wpdb->prepare("INSERT INTO
130.                          `architect_contacts` (`full_name`, `email`)
131.                          VALUES (%s, %s )",
132.                      $full_name, $email)
133.                  );
134.                  $uniq_token = arch_unique_token();
135.                  arch_send_welcome_email($email, $uniq_token, $full_name);
136.                  $contacts_widget_return_message =
137.                      "<p class='saved_message'>Contact Information saved...<br/>Check your email to
    confirm<br/>Thanks for joining us!</p>";
138.              }
139.          } //end if already exists test
140.      } else {
141.          // end data intergity fail tests
142.          $contacts_widget_return_message =
143.              "<p class='error_message'>" . $contacts_widget_return_message . "</p>";
144.      }
145.
146.      // show message on widget area
147.      return $contacts_widget_return_message;
148.  } // end public_save method
149.
150. } // end of class definition
```

It object-oriented programming code, and the class defined is based upon the WP_Widget[22] class provided by WordPress.

```
class architect_contacts_widget extends WP_Widget {
// ...
 }
```

Your task is to build the form which appears within the sidebar and manages the code that saves the data back to the database. Everything else can extend from this WP_Widget class. The code for a form that collects the data on the public side (Figure 5.8) is in the method called widget(). The code to manage the collected data—data sanitation, integrity checking, and database storage—is in the public_save() method. Also note that the form() method creates the widget block that can be inserted into the sidebars on the admin widgets page, shown earlier in Figure 5.7. The __construct() method on our extended class also loads the following custom CSS in a file called arch-widget.css stored in the CSS folder.

```
submit_btn {
    background: #008ec2 !important;
    border-color: #006799 !important;
    color: #fff !important;
}
```

Doing this allows for custom formatting of the output of the widget form. We have a class named submit_btn added to the form submit button, and our CSS can affect here if desired. Note that we elected to use "!important" in our CSS file for these settings to be taken into account because the parent class of this object has its CSS pre-loaded. You could also simply leave your CSS classes or IDs unaltered and allow the plugin user to change the settings with their CSS. If you are going to do that, you need to ensure your classes and IDs are uniquely named so the plugin user can be accurate in how they make their custom CSS.

Calling the newly created widget into existence is accomplished with the familiar add_action() function within the main plugin file, architect-subscribers.php, and using the widgets_init hook. The second parameter to this action is to call a function we create that uses the register_widget() function within it.

It's important to note here that the parameter passed to the register_widget() function has to be the same name used in the class definition in the OOP required code file. This makes the connection between the widget's definition and its code. Then, of course, we need to include the Widget class code file with the require_once function from the architect-subscribers.php main file. The full code is shown here:

---

[22] WP_Widget: *https://phpa.me/wpdev-wp-widget*

```
add_action('widgets_init', 'architect_register_contacts_widget');

function architect_register_contacts_widget() {
    // parameter is the class name in following required file
    register_widget('architect_contacts_widget');
}

require_once(ARCHITECT_PLUGIN_FILEPATH_INCLUDES . "architect-contacts-widget.php");
```

Google ReCAPTCHA

You may also want to add a CAPTCHA ("Completely Automated Public Turing test to tell computers and humans apart") to the public forms where you collect information. It's another method that helps safeguard data collection integrity by ensuring the data entry does not come from a bot or another spammy data entry method. It tries to ensure a human is filling out the form.

Google makes one of the most effective and widespread CAPTCHAs; they call it "Google reCAPTCHA." There are four versions available at the time of this writing, and the version 2 check-box version is better for form data collection. You can read this version and how the three versions[23] differ in the online documentation. See Figure 5.9 as an example of what this reCAPTCHA looks like.

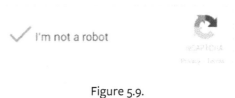

Figure 5.9.

To invoke this additional safeguard on the form, we need to add code before the form and at the location on the form where we want the Google reCAPTCHA to appear. Since we may potentially use this many times, we have added this to our list of reusable functions we keep in our architect-functions.php file included in the main plugin file. The architect-functions.php file is shown in Listing 5.10.

Listing 5.10.

```
1. <?php
2. /* =========================== */
3. /* send out welcome email function */
4. /* =========================== */
5. function arch_send_welcome_email($email, $token, $full_name) {
6.
7.     $confirm_url = add_query_arg(array('arch_subscribe'=>$token), get_site_url());
```

---

[23] three versions: https://phpa.me/recaptcha-versions

```php
8.
9.      $subject = 'Architect PHP - Please confirm your signup';
10.
11.     $message = "Hi $full_name: <br/><br/>Thanks for joining our newsletter sign up process. ";
12.     $message .= "<br/><strong>[If this was not you please ignore this email]</strong><br/>";
13.     $message .= "<br/>Please follow this link to confirm your subscription to our email notification list: <br/> ";
14.     $message .= "<a href='$confirm_url'> Confirm sign up </a>";
15.
16.     // Send email to new sign up email.
17.     $headers = array('Content-Type: text/html; charset=UTF-8');
18.     wp_mail( $email, $subject, $message, $headers );
19. } // end send_welcome_email function
20.
21. /* ======================================== */
22. /* generate unique ID for new subscriber function */
23. /* ======================================== */
24. function arch_unique_token() {
25.     global $wpdb;
26.     $result = $wpdb->get_row( $wpdb->prepare("SELECT `token_prefix`
27.         FROM `architect_control` WHERE `architect_control_id` = %d", 1 )
28.     );
29.     $prefix = $result->token_prefix ;
30.     return uniqid($prefix, true) ;
31. }
32.
33. /* ========================= */
34. /* Build help icon and title text */
35. /* ========================= */
36. function arch_build_help($field) {
37.     global $wpdb;
38.     $image_source = ARCHITECT_PLUGIN_URL . 'images/question_mark.png' ;
39.
40.     $result_help = $wpdb->get_row( $wpdb->prepare("SELECT architect_help_help AS help_text
41.         FROM `architect_help` WHERE `architect_help_field` = %s", $field) );
42.     if ($result_help) {
43.         $out_string = "<img src='$image_source' title='$result_help->help_text' />" ;
44.     } else {
45.         $out_string = "" ;
46.     }
47.     return $out_string ;
48. }
49. /* ================= */
50. /* Build ReCaptcha top */
51. /* ================= */
52. function arch_build_recaptcha_top() {
53.     echo "<script src='https://www.google.com/recaptcha/api.js' async defer></script>";
54.     return ;
55. }
```

```
56.  /* ================= */
57.  /* Build ReCaptcha main */
58.  /* ================= */
59.  function arch_build_recaptcha_main() {
60.      global $wpdb;
61.      $result_rc = $wpdb->get_row( $wpdb->prepare("SELECT `grc_site_key`
62.              FROM `architect_control` WHERE `architect_control_id` = %d", 1 )
63.      );
64.      $site_key = $result_rc->grc_site_key ;
65.      echo "<tr class='TableOverride'><td> </td><td ><br/>";
66.      echo "<div class='g-recaptcha' data-sitekey='" . $site_key . "'></div>";
67.      echo "</td></tr>";
68.      return ;
69.  }
70.  /* ================= */
71.  /* Verify ReCaptcha response */
72.  /* ================= */
73.  function arch_verify_recaptcha($action) {
74.      global $wpdb;
75.      $result_rc = $wpdb->get_row( $wpdb->prepare("SELECT `grc_secret_key`
76.              FROM `architect_control` WHERE `architect_control_id` = %d", 1 )
77.      );
78.      $secret_key = $result_rc->grc_secret_key ;
79.      $url = 'https://www.google.com/recaptcha/api/siteverify';
80.      $data = array(
81.              'secret' => $secret_key,
82.              'response' => $action
83.      );
84.      $options = array(
85.              'http' => array (
86.                      'method' => 'POST',
87.                      'content' => http_build_query($data)
88.              )
89.      );
90.      $context = stream_context_create($options);
91.      $verify = file_get_contents($url, false, $context);
92.      $captcha_success = json_decode($verify);
93.      if ($captcha_success->success == false) {
94.          $response = false;
95.      } else if ($captcha_success->success==true) {
96.          $response = true;
97.      }
98.      return $response ;
99.  }
```

Keep in mind this reCAPTCHA requires a site key and a secret key generated by Google after you register your website with them. In all likelihood, you would need a place within your plugin's settings page to allow your plugin user to store their

> *generated keys. This means extending the settings page and the underlying database table, as well. Take another look at Figure 5.6 to see that part of the data entry form.*

The code to display the reCAPTCHA by calling these functions is provided in Listing 5.11; the specific functions to build the reCAPTCHA parts are shown below for convenience.

Listing 5.11.

```
1.  function arch_build_recaptcha_top()
2.  {
3.      echo "<script src='https://www.google.com/recaptcha/api.js' async defer></script>";
4.  }
5.
6.  function arch_build_recaptcha_main()
7.  {
8.      echo "<tr class='TableOverride'><td> </td><td ><br/>";
9.      echo "<div class='g-recaptcha' data-sitekey='6LfgFY8UA********F8rMR'></div>";
10.     echo "</td></tr>";
11. }
```

Figure 5.10 shows the code function calls and where they should be inserted in the form page in the widget method of the class. The first call should be before the `<form>` tag, and the second should be before the submit button or wherever you want the reCAPTCHA block to appear.

Take another look at Figure 5.8 to see the reCAPTCHA displayed on the public widget form.

```
// display the widget
function widget ($args, $instance) {
    extract($args);
    echo $before_widget;
    $title = apply_filters ('widget_title', $instance['title']);
    if (!empty($title) ) { echo $before_title . $title . $after_title; } ;
    arch_build_recaptcha_top();
    ?>
    <form action="" method="post" >

    <p> Full Name: <input type="text" class="widefat" name="full_name" value="" /></p>

    <p> eMail: <input type="text" class="widefat" name="email" value="" /></p>

    <?php arch_build_recaptcha_main(); ?>
    </br>
    <input type="submit" name="submit" class="submit_btn" value="Join List" >

    <?php wp_nonce_field('nonce_action', 'nonce_field') ;

    // check that the form was submitted
    if(isset($_POST['submit']) && $_POST['submit'] == "Join List" ) {
        echo $this->public_save($_POST);
    } ?>
    </form>
```

Figure 5.10.

Creating A Dashboard Widget

A Dashboard widget is another feature you may see from time to time on a WordPress plugin. These are informational panels that can be shown on the overall administration Dashboard shown when an admin user first logs in. WordPress has a few of these already in place by default such as "Quick Draft", "At a Glance", and "WordPress Events and News."

Figure 5.11.

You can create a dashboard widget to make announcements specific to your plugins if so desired. Figure 5.11 shows a basic dashboard widget we created for our sample plugin.

Here we show a dashboard box title of "Architect Free Plugin Info" with some helpful text in red. The code to create this is an add_action() call with the hook of wp_dashboard_setup. The second parameter is a function to call with another function call within it. The inner function call is wp_add_dashboard_widget(). One of the parameters of this inner function is a reference to the dashboard box's inner content. This can be a lot of code brought in by a call to the require() function, or as in our case, just displaying some text. Listing 5.12 shows the full code snippet.

Listing 5.12.

```
1. add_action('wp_dashboard_setup', 'architect_dashboard_sample');
2.
3. function architect_dashboard_sample()
4. {
5.    wp_add_dashboard_widget('dashboard_custom_feed', 'Architect Free Plugin Info',
6.       'arch_dashboard_display');
7. }
8.
9. function arch_dashboard_display()
10. {
11.    echo "<font color=red>Architect Plugin Demo - help is on the way! </font>";
12. }
```

Troubleshooting And Debug Tools

Your plugin can get quite complicated as it evolves, and you add features. Think of WooCommerce, or Shareaholic, and its complexities. When you are building a plugin, you will undoubtedly get into the deep weeds. You may need additional help in sorting things out like, considering some of the WordPress/PHP warnings or errors that could be generated and making sure your SQL is correct and not too resource-intensive.

Thankfully, WordPress has a development plugin that reports on conditions within your code and the WordPress environment to help you debug at a reasonable depth. This plugin is called "Debug Bar."[24] We are currently warned this plugin has not been updated for a long time, so be sure to use it with caution. There are other complementary plugins you can also use with Debug Bar; one, in particular, is "Query Monitor"[25]. These two plugins alone can save you a lot of developmental headaches. Debug Bar, when activated, looks like Figure 5.12 with notices and warnings displayed. It also has a menu of its own where you can see other debug subjects like recent query results and the object cache.

Figure 5.12.

With Query Monitor turned on and activated, you see an additional panel open up—usually on the lower half of the screen—showing more of any recent activity on your WordPress site. Figure 5.13 shows a sample of what this might look like. Be sure to explore these two plugins to see what other interrogation information they can provide.

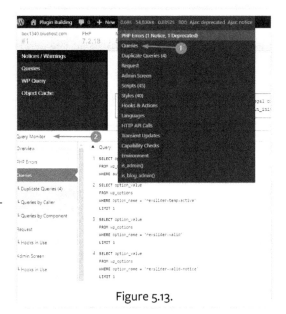

Figure 5.13.

---

[24] "Debug Bar.": https://wordpress.org/plugins/debug-bar/
[25] "Query Monitor": https://wordpress.org/plugins/query-monitor/

Installation And Update Processes

There are two principal parts to finishing your plugin and releasing it on the WordPress ecosystem. One that we are looking at in this section is how it should install and update itself. The second part we will look at in the following section is how to distribute your plugin.

Looking at the installation of your plugin, we need to be aware that two specific tasks need to exist. One for the initial installation of the plugin on any WordPress site, and the other is how it updates itself on subsequent releases. We can code these tasks in the same file, which we must name [plugin-name]_activation.php. It should reside in the /includes folder. Replace [plugin-name] with the actual name or reference of the plugin; in our case, it would be architect-activation.php.

One thing you must consider when you are initially installing a plugin is what minimum version of WordPress your plugin supports. This can be done with the following code placed at the top of the activation code file:

```
if (version_compare(get_bloginfo('version'),'5.0','<')) {
    // deactivate the  plugin if current WordPress version is less than that noted above
    deactivate_plugins(basename(__FILE__));
    exit("Your WordPress Version is too old for this plugin...") ;
}
```

Here, we test to see if WordPress's current version is < less than 5.0. If the test fails, your WordPress version is 4.8, for example, then we deactivate the plugin and exit the installation process with a message that the current version is too old. You can set the version value to whatever number you want, but try to keep it a relatively current version so that your plugin can be used with the latest version and features of WordPress.

The next aspect of the plugin setup process are the steps taken when you update a plugin with new or changed features. The update process, and it happens every time the plugin update procedure runs.

Any code you write for this process should run immediately after the version level test runs. So any code changes or database changes should be placed in the update file right after the installation version test to ensure it always executes when you update the plugin. The function that calls this process is register_activation_hook, and you should place it in the main plugin code file. This function fires every time a plugin is either installed or updated. This is different from an add_action call since you only want this code to happen at these two special times. The code to call these processes into action is as follows:

```
register_activation_hook(__FILE__, 'arch_activation_code');

function arch_activation_code(){
    require_once(ARCHITECT_PLUGIN_FILEPATH_INCLUDES . "architect-activation.php");
}
```

A sample activation code file is provided here, in Listing 5.13 Note the use of the dbDelta() function when dealing with custom database tables. This function manages any table changes and subsequent data alterations for you, so custom table updates are performed smoothly.

Listing 5.13.

```
1.  <?php
2.  // check WordPress version requirements
3.  if (version_compare(get_bloginfo('version'), '5.0', '<')) {
4.      //   deactivate the  plugin if current WordPress version is less than that noted above
5.      deactivate_plugins(basename(__FILE__));
6.      exit("Your WordPress Version is too old for this plugin...");
7.  }
8.
9.  global $wpdb;
10.
11. require_once(ABSPATH . 'wp-admin/includes/upgrade.php');
12.
13. /* =============================== */
14. /* Create architect_control table    */
15. /* =============================== */
16.
17. $architect_sql = "CREATE TABLE `architect_control` (
18.    `architect_control_id` int(11) NOT NULL AUTO_INCREMENT,
19.    `email_updates` tinyint(4) NOT NULL,
20.    `token_prefix` varchar(10) NOT NULL,
21.    `grc_site_key` VARCHAR(75) NOT NULL,
22.    `grc_secret_key` VARCHAR(75) NOT NULL,
23.    PRIMARY KEY (`architect_control_id`) ) ";
24. dbDelta($architect_sql);
25. /* ==================================== */
26. /* seed table with control row and basic  */
27. /* data if there is no existing row       */
28. /* ==================================== */
29.
30. $row_exists = $wpdb->get_var($wpdb->prepare("SELECT `architect_control_id` FROM `architect_control`
31.        WHERE `architect_control_id` = %d", 1));
32. if (!$row_exists) {
33.    $wpdb->query($wpdb->prepare("INSERT INTO `architect_control`
34.        (`architect_control_id`, `email_updates`)
35.        VALUES (%d, %d)", 1, 1));
36. }
```

```
37. /* ================================= */
38. /* Create architect_contacts table   */
39. /* ================================= */
40.
41. $architect_sql = "CREATE TABLE `architect_contacts` (
42.   `architect_contacts_id` int(11) NOT NULL AUTO_INCREMENT,
43.   `architect_token` VARCHAR(33) NOT NULL,
44.   `full_name` varchar(100) NOT NULL,
45.   `email` varchar(100) NOT NULL,
46.   `email_confirmed` tinyint(4) NOT NULL DEFAULT '0',
47.   `email_optin_ip` varchar(50) NOT NULL,
48.   `email_optin_date` varchar(10) NOT NULL,
49.   PRIMARY KEY (`architect_contacts_id`) ) ";
50. dbDelta($architect_sql);
51.
52. /* ==============================*/
53. /* Create architect_help table   */
54. /* ==============================*/
55.
56. $architect_sql = "CREATE TABLE `architect_help` (
57. `architect_help_id` INT NOT NULL AUTO_INCREMENT ,
58. `architect_help_field` VARCHAR(75) NULL ,
59. `architect_help_help` TEXT NULL ,
60. PRIMARY KEY (`architect_help_id`))";
61. dbDelta($architect_sql);
62. /* ==================================== */
63. /* seed table with control row and basic  */
64. /* data if there is no existing row       */
65. /* ==================================== */
66.
67. $row_exists = $wpdb->get_var($wpdb->prepare("SELECT `architect_help_id` FROM `architect_help`
68.         WHERE `architect_help_id` = %d", 1));
69. if (!$row_exists) {
70.   $wpdb->query($wpdb->prepare("INSERT INTO `architect_help`
71.     (`architect_help_field`, `architect_help_help`) VALUES (%s, %s)",
72.     "token_prefix", "This is used to make the opt-in email link unique, so that we can know better where
    the link is coming from."));
73. }
74. /* ==================================== */
75. /* build email confirmation page if needed */
76. /* ==================================== */
77.
78. $new_page_title = 'eMail Confirmation';
79. $new_page_content = 'email-confirmed ... thanks for that !';
80. $new_page_template = '';
81. $page_check = get_page_by_title($new_page_title);
82. $new_page = [
83.   'post_type' => 'page',
84.   'post_title' => $new_page_title,
85.   'post_content' => $new_page_content,
86.   'post_status' => 'publish',
87.   'post_author' => 1,
88. ];
```

```
 89. if (!isset($page_check->ID)) {
 90.     $new_page_id = wp_insert_post($new_page);
 91.     if (!empty($new_page_template)) {
 92.         update_post_meta($new_page_id, '_wp_page_template', $new_page_template);
 93.     }
 94. }
 95. /* =============================================== */
 96. /* build email unsubscribe confirmation page if needed */
 97. /* =============================================== */
 98.
 99. $new_page_title = 'eMail Unsubscribe';
100. $new_page_content =
101.   'You have been unsubscribed from the email list ... sorry to see you go.';
102. $new_page_template = '';
103. $page_check = get_page_by_title($new_page_title);
104. $new_page = [
105.     'post_type' => 'page',
106.     'post_title' => $new_page_title,
107.     'post_content' => $new_page_content,
108.     'post_status' => 'publish',
109.     'post_author' => 1,
110. ];
111. if (!isset($page_check->ID)) {
112.     $new_page_id = wp_insert_post($new_page);
113.     if (!empty($new_page_template)) {
114.         update_post_meta($new_page_id, '_wp_page_template', $new_page_template);
115.     }
116. }
```

Removing The Plugin

The reverse of this process is also essential to consider. What actions do you want to take when someone deactivates and deletes your plugin? It's regarded as a best practice to "clean up after yourself" by removing all traces of your plugin when it is deleted. The WordPress uninstall process removes all the plugin code and folders related to the plugin. However, it is also a best practice—or at least a courtesy—to ask your plugin users if they want to save data before it's deleted.

These deletion steps can all be done if you add code to the uninstall.php file that should be present as part of the plugin. Any code in this file runs automatically once the deletion process is activated correctly. Many plugins leave data behind in the database. The thinking here is to leave the data behind in case the user ever re-installs the plugin. Worst case, the plugin developer forgot to implement this step. A better way is to offer the user a data backup option, and a data restore option if they do indeed choose to re-install. Also, be sure to take into account any issues with your plugin and its data related to GDPR or other privacy laws you have to follow.

At the very least, you should have this line of code in your `uninstall.php` file:

```
if (!defined('WP_UNINSTALL_PLUGIN')) exit() ;
```

This clause ensures an admin user did indeed trigger the WordPress uninstall process and it was not called directly by mistake. Trying to remember to add the deletion code at the end of a development project can be painful. One approach is to add code to this uninstall file as you create the overall plugin—if it relies on custom tables—by adding the DROP TABLE commands as you develop your plugin. You can see this in Listing 5.14, where we drop three of our custom tables.

Listing 5.14.

```php
 1. <?php
 2. /* =============================================== */
 3. /* if the constant is not defined then get out ! */
 4. /* =============================================== */
 5. if (!defined('WP_UNINSTALL_PLUGIN')) {
 6.    exit() ;
 7. }
 8.
 9. /* ====================================== */
10. // Drop the DB tables related to the plugin */
11. /* ====================================== */
12. global $wpdb;
13.
14. $wpdb->query('DROP TABLE architect_contacts');
15. $wpdb->query('DROP TABLE architect_control');
16. $wpdb->query('DROP TABLE architect_help');
```

Distributing Your Plugins

Naturally, the ultimate point of creating a plugin is to get it out to the masses. We can distribute plugins in two ways: commercially a paid product or via WordPress.org. Commercially means it is available on your site or a commercial website like Theme Forest[26] but not on WordPress.org. Commercially, in this context, does not necessarily mean for money. Instead, it is used to describe the alternate method of distributing your plugin via WordPress.org.

---

[26] *Theme Forest: https://themeforest.net*

Commercially

If you want to distribute your plugin separately from WordPress.org, you have to bundle all of the plugin files including the plugin's home folder into a ZIP file. Distributing this file on any web platform and having the ZIP file available for download is sufficient. If

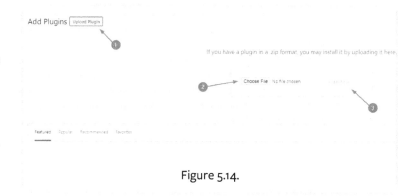

Figure 5.14.

you want to either sell it or give it away, you can do either via this method. The plugin user would then have to download the ZIP file and go through the installation process within the WordPress admin area for plugin setup and select the ZIP file as an upload file. Figure 5.14 shows this screen in the admin area.

The caveat here is that any updates must be done manually since no update announcements are made within the built-in WordPress ecosystem. You should create an email announcement list or provide a notification within a dashboard widget to announce plugin updates as they become available.

Via WordPress.org

The other method of distributing your plugin is through the WordPress.org system. Here you have to upload your plugin code for the WordPress folks to review, and then you have to add the files through their SVN version control system. By distributing it here, you must make it open source via a license compatible with the Gnu Public License v2. Doing so allows anyone to download, view, edit, and redistribute the plugin's source code. To learn more, start with the FAQ[27] provided by the Open Source Initiative.

> *Although any GPL-compatible license is acceptable, using the same license as WordPress—"GPLv2 or later"—is strongly recommended.*

To submit your plugin for review, you need to have a WordPress.org account, and then you can go to this page to start the process[28]. Besides having an update process in place, as mentioned in the previous section, you also need to have a readme.txt file that describes the

---

[27] *FAQ:* https://opensource.org/faq
[28] *start the process:* https://wordpress.org/plugins/developers/add/

plugin and any of its major features. The guide to creating a readme.txt file is here[29]. This was also briefly discussed earlier in the chapter in the Basic Files and Folder Layout section.

Summary

There are many nuances to creating a plugin, and we have covered most of them in this chapter. If you want to dig deeper, you should read the entire plugin writing guide[30]. Our next chapter guides you in creating a child theme from a parent theme. You can extend themes in this way to customize them to do exactly what you want. Following that chapter, we will look at ways to internationalize your plugins to make them useful in many languages.

---

[29] here: https://phpa.me/wp-readme-works
[30] plugin writing guide: https://codex.wordpress.org/Writing_a_Plugin

Chapter
6

Child Themes

Building a WordPress site involves creating or customizing a theme. To begin, we need to understand a WordPress theme is the public part of a website; in other words, the "view layer."

Why Build A Child Theme?

The view layer includes logic related to posts and makes decisions like how and when to present a post or a part of it. Because the presentation is sophisticated and capable of evolving, you need to revisit it frequently. Once you have a new theme available, you should customize it according to your project goals. How you customize it might affect your project's future, causing future decisions to become irreversible and blocking updates of the original theme.

WordPress allows you to override behavior in a parent theme by creating a child theme[1]. The parent theme can be one of the WordPress default themes, a theme provided by a third party, or even your custom starter theme. It can vary from a single `style.css` file to a large number of pages and extra functionalities. The main advantages of using a child theme are:

- Maintainability and safe theme updates—separating your custom code to a child theme keeps the parent theme updatable
- Safe fallback—the parent theme handles provides functionalities not covered by custom development
- Extensibility—working with child themes allows you to add new functionality or customize existing ones without changing the parent theme.

Some might ask if a plugin with some CSS customizations can accomplish the same goal; it works if you're limited to a few style changes. The fact is, there are many ways of doing the same thing with WordPress. However, they may differ in terms of maintainability. For example, it might be hard to find code that customizes a style because it's stored within a file called `ajax_handlers.php`. When we talk about maintainability here, we mean how well documented and organized your customizations are in regards to your project goals. If you want to change a few CSS aspects of your theme, your best choice is to override the CSS directly in the child theme.

Child themes are recommended for the following:

- Changes to small pieces of the parent theme.
- Customizations to the parent theme's template files output.
- Augmenting the output of the parent theme's functions.

---

[1] child theme: _https://phpa.me/wpdev-child-themes_

Customizing The Twenty Nineteen Theme

We'll be using a popular WordPress theme—Twenty Nineteen—in our example of customizing a theme. Out of the box, Twenty Nineteen has a lot of functionality and many WordPress features. WordPress themes are comprised of templates. We cover the ones that are frequently affected by the template hierarchy principles later in this chapter. If you want to know more about WordPress template files, visit the WordPress documentation, which covers them in more detail[2].

Step One: Theme Folder

The first step is to add your child theme file. In the themes directory, `wp-content/themes`, where our original theme is, create another directory with the same name of the original theme and append "-child" to its name. Our theme that extends Twenty Nineteen will be called `twentynineteen-child`. This naming convention is a recommended practice for organizing your themes, not a requirement, but it does help keep your child themes with their parent. Once done, we have two directories in `wp-content/themes`:

1. `twentynineteen`
2. `twentynineteen-child`

Step Two: Stylesheet

To find themes and child themes, WordPress scans for metadata. We can place this information in the `style.css` file we use to override the parent's CSS.

Now that we have the child theme directory, create the file `style.css`. At the beginning of this file, add the code shown in Listing 6.1.

Listing 6.1.

```
1.  /*
2.  Theme Name:    My Twenty Nineteen Child Theme
3.  Theme URI:     https://myawesomewebsite.com/my-twenty-nineteeen-child-theme/
4.  Description:   This is my first Child Theme.
5.  Author:        John Doe
6.  Author URI:    https://myawesomewebsite.com
7.  Template:      twentynineteen
8.  Version:       1.0.0
9.  License:       GNU General Public License v2 or later
10. License URI:   http://www.gnu.org/licenses/gpl-2.0.html
11. Tags:          custom-background, custom-logo, custom-menu, featured-images,
    threaded-comments, translation-ready
12. Text Domain:   twentynineteenchild
13. */
```

---

[2]   more detail: *https://phpa.me/wpdev-basics-template*

Fill in the information as shown. Your child theme is now ready, but the only thing it does is replace the parent's stylesheet with this empty one.

Your child theme is now available for activation. Go to Administration Screen > Appearance > Themes and activate the theme named "My Twenty Nineteen Child Theme." The activated theme does not have any styling. Another step is necessary to link the parent theme's CSS.

> **Note**: *Adding custom branding information is a small detail that may help your work appear more professional. The stylesheet comment we added includes some information about this child theme; you can customize all that information. It displays in the theme's information on the selection page. You can customize the screenshot located there by adding an image called* `screenshot.png` *to the root of the child theme's directory.*

Step Three: Parent CSS

Next, we have to enqueue the styles properly. You may have noticed the parent theme's `style.css` file was replaced completely by the child theme's `style.css`. To include the parent theme's style, we have two options:

Option One—Enqueue Style

The most common option is to enqueue the style in your child theme's `functions.php` file. To do this, create a `functions.php` file in your child theme folder. Note that `functions.php`, unlike `style.css`, does not override the parent theme.

To include the parent's stylesheet when this child theme is loaded, your functions file should look like Listing 6.2:

Listing 6.2.

```
1. <?php
2.
3. /**
4. * Add parent's theme
5. */
6. add_action( 'wp_enqueue_scripts', 'twentynineteen_child_enqueue_styles' );
7. if ( ! function_exists( 'twentynineteen_child_enqueue_styles' ) ) {
8.    function twentynineteen_child_enqueue_styles() {
9.        wp_enqueue_style( 'parent-style', get_template_directory_uri() . '/style.css' );
10.   }
11. }
```

Always remember to check whether the function exists before declaring it. Doing so is essential in WordPress environments to avoid conflicts with other WordPress plugin's possible function names. Note we are following our guideline to prepend function names, in this case, with the `twentynineteen_child_` to match our theme name.

Option Two—Include The Parent Theme's Stylesheet

The second option is to use the CSS import rule. This rule is well supported in modern browsers and has been supported by Internet Explorer since version 5.5. To use the CSS import rule, add the following code after any `@charset` declaration, but before everything else. This line goes in your child theme's `style.css` file.

```
@import url("../twentynineteen/style.css");
```

The WordPress documentation, as of the writing of this book, was not updated to cover all possible cases. The inclusion of the stylesheet depends on how the parent theme includes its stylesheet. We will cover a few of these cases after the current steps and the section "Considerations About Including Child Theme Stylesheet," where two additional conditions will be covered.

Step Four: Customize Theme

Now, let's customize our child theme to confirm that our child theme is working correctly. The typical UI of a website using the Twenty Nineteen theme looks like the one in Figure 6.1.

Let's add the following lines to the `style.css` file we created in the second step:

```
h2.entry-title {
  color: blue;
}
```

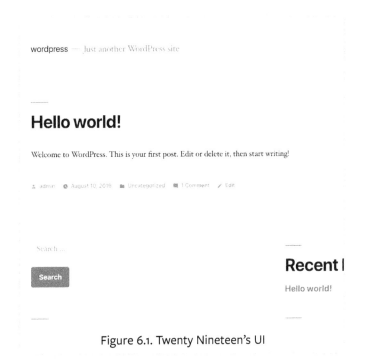

Figure 6.1. Twenty Nineteen's UI

This code causes the header to be blue, as in Figure 6.2. If you don't see a change, ensure the child stylesheet loads after the parent's CSS file.

If it matches, congratulations, the customization through the child theme worked correctly.

Customizing Themes With The Child Themes Strategy

To customize any part of our theme, we can copy that specific file. For the theme in question, to update the header, we copy the header.php file. The same thing applies to any other part of the child theme.

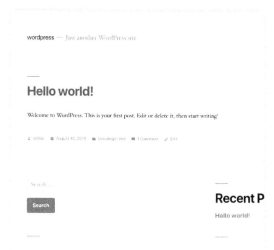

Figure 6.2. Twenty Nineteen with blue header

To customize themes properly, you need to understand the template hierarchy. It provides all of the information you need to customize your themes.

Many well-known plugins use the strategy of relying on child themes to make it easy for developers to customize their frontend pages. One example is WooCommerce, which can be customized as you would a child theme. In your active theme, create a folder named woocommerce. There, you can override any template WooCommerce has in its templates" directory (wp-content/plugins/woocommerce/templates`). To do this, copy the templates that you want to customize into your theme and update the new copies.

The WooCommerce documentation provides a Theme Developer Handbook[3] where you can learn more about how to use this in the WooCommerce environment.

Template Hierarchy

When rendering theme output, WordPress picks the most specific template available. With that in mind, the template hierarchy gives us the following query strategy to select which template file to use.

First, the system matches the type of the page. Next, the system looks for the most specific template following the template hierarchy. Whenever WordPress can't find a file, it scans further up the hierarchy.

---

[3] Theme Developer Handbook: https://phpa.me/woocommerce-theme-dev

Figure 6.3. Template Hierarchy

The template hierarchy follows the strategy expressed in Figure 6.3

This image is from the Template Hierarchy[4] page in the WordPress Codex.

Let's consider an example. When you request a page, WordPress first tries to find any reference to an object (e.g., category, post, object, page). If the request is for an object, the system looks for a matching file name, in this order:

1. For a *slug* in the URL (e.g., `category-{slug}.php`),
2. for an ID (e.g., `category-{id}.php`),
3. for the object's core page (e.g., `category.php`, `author.php`, `taxonomy.php`), and finally,
4. for the fallback page (e.g., `archive.php`, `single.php`, `page.php`).
5. If none of these files exists, the system uses `index.php`.

---

[4] *Template Hierarchy: https://phpa.me/wpdev-template-hierarchy*

The base of the templating organization handles the following functionalities:

- Front page
- Post types—Taxonomies
- Authors
- Search

For each functionality, we have a custom handling strategy that follows similar specificity rules. There are a few different ways of accomplishing the same things; we will cover the basics. You can find a more precise method of doing in the diagram in Figure 6.3 or in the core WordPress Theme documentation[5].

The following is a summary to promote a better understanding of the logic behind the fallbacks for the basic WordPress objects, post, and page post types.

Front Page

The front-page.php template is the page shown when someone accesses the website's root navigation (http://example.com/). The next file in the sequence is home.php. This sequence might be affected by the settings at the Settings > Reading section, if the template page.php is used when "a static page" is selected. David Sutoyo has a more detailed explanation of the difference between frontpage and home[6], but here is the basic Reading Settings behavior.

The WordPress setting to configure this hierarchy behavior is "Your homepage displays." There you have two options: "Your latest posts" or "A static page." as in Figure 6.4.

When you select "Your latest posts," the file home.php is used first. When you choose "A static page," you have two options to customize "Homepage" and "Post Pages;" front-page.php is used first. The options for "Homepage" customize which file is

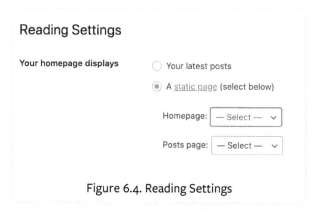

Figure 6.4. Reading Settings

used if front-page.php is not available (e.g., it uses something-page.php if such a file exists and "something" is selected here). The option "Post Pages" specifies which file to use for blog pages (e.g., when accessing the address /articles).

---

[5] Theme documentation: https://developer.wordpress.org/themes/
[6] frontpage and home: https://phpa.me/sutuyo-front-vs-home

Post And Custom Post Types

Every asset maintained by WordPress is essentially a custom post type. For a store, the "product records" is usually a "product." The media uploaded to your website are post types named "attachment." Knowing that, can explore different ways of serving this content to the user within your theme you.

When a single record is accessed, the invoked template is `single-{post-type}-{slug}.php` (e.g., `single-post-my-awesome-post.php`). The next in the hierarchy is `single-{post-type}.php`. To customize a "product" post type page for all products, we create a file called `single-product.php` (this follows the structure `single-{post-type}.php`).

You can also customize how a single product displays. For a product with the slug `my-awesome-product` create a template named `single-product-my-awesome-product.php`. The filename follows the structure `single-{post-type}-{slug}.php`. If WordPress doesn't pick up a custom template, double check that you didn't typo or misspell a part of the filename.

There is an alternative method to the post slug: the post ID. As an example, this template file could be named `single-product-1.php`. That is more limited, and you have to make sure when moving your website to another server (e.g., production server) that the system uses the same ID for the post—something that might not be trivial.

Page

The `page` post type has particular behavior. It uses `page.php` instead of `single-` in the hierarchy. Additionally, they have extra support only allowed to them: templates. Templates are considered page attributes and determine which template file WordPress calls when loading the page. The WordPress admin user at the page editor controls the template.

A page template does not follow the same rules the rest of the templates do when directly set to a WordPress page. They bypass the WordPress page hierarchy and use the specified file when invoking that page.

When using Gutenberg, you can pick it, as shown in Figure 6.5.

When using the Classic Editor, the field is shown in Figure 6.6.

To create a page template, copy the file `page.php` that exists in any default WordPress theme and add this comment to the top:

```php
<?php /* Template Name: Template One */ ?>
```

Figure 6.5. Template for Page Block Editor

Figure 6.6. Template selection for Page Classic Editor

Creating A Page Template

Let's make a test implementing a page template in five steps.

1. Create a copy of the file `page.php` from the parent theme, naming it `page-template-one.php`.

2. Change the Template Name at the top of this file, before everything else.

3. Add the following code right after `get_header(); ?>`:

```
<div>My confirmation mark.</div>
```

4. When editing a page in the admin, confirm the new template is available in the template options as in Figure 6.7.

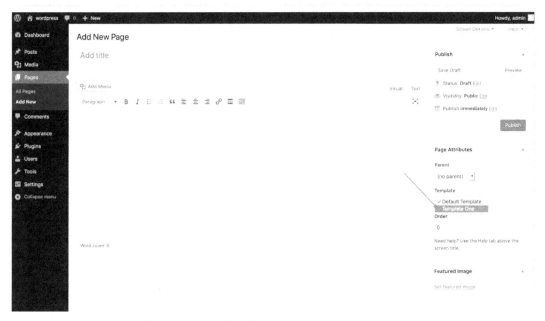

Figure 6.7. Template One as a page template option

5. After selecting the specific template, and saving it, you should see the following (Figure 6.8) on the frontend of the website.

Figure 6.8. See the template in the front end

Quick Reference

This section serves as a quick reference for following the hierarchy in a simplified tree perspective. Here we have the Categories such as "Front Page", "Post Types", and "Taxonomies." After that, you'll find the actual files of the subgroups that WordPress calls in hierarchy sequence.

- **Front Page**:
  - front-page.php
  - home.php
  - page.php
- **Post Types**:
  - Page:
    - custom template file (defined by the "page template functionality")
    - page-{slug}.php
    - page-{id}.php
    - page.php
    - singular.php

- Attachment:
  - {MIME-type}.php (e.g.: text-plain.php)
  - attachment.php
  - single-attachment-{slug}.php
  - single.php
  - singular.php
- Generic Post Types:
  - single-{post-type}-{slug}.php
  - single-{post_type}.php
  - single.php
  - singular.php
- **Taxonomies**:
  - Tag, Category:
    - {category|tag}-{slug}.php
    - {category|tag}-{id}.php
    - {category|tag}.php
    - archive.php
- Generic Taxonomy:
  - taxonomy-{taxonomy}-{term}.php
  - taxonomy-{taxonomy}.php
  - taxonomy.php
  - archive.php
- **Authors**:
  - author-{nicename}.php
  - author-{id}.php
  - author.php
  - archive.php
- **Search**:
  - search.php

All of these templates fall back to index.php if they are not in your theme or parent.

Chapter

7

Internationalization

Since WordPress's reach is global, it makes sense to allow as many people and languages to use your plugin creations. Creating a plugin multi-language enabled is one of the more useful features you can add to it.

The preferred approach is to build your plugin with international features while you are writing the code for it. However, it may be challenging to do that while keeping other best practices in mind, like security. It would be understandable if you left the translation to a later phase of development. You can even be forgiven if you don't add it until after you release the initial version of your plugin in English.

The first aspect of internationalization (i.e., making your plugin multilingual) is to be conscious of where you want the language options to appear. Do you have in-line help text? Do you have form fields or form labels? These are a few of the considerations to be made. Each aspect of displayable text can be handled a little differently, so it's best to plan ahead. To be clear, we're focusing on translating the UI elements for our example plugin. Internationalizing is a broad topic, and it can touch on managing versions of your content in multiple languages[1].

Here, we translate the sample plugin we started in Chapter 5. We translate the settings page's text and displayed help message to Italian, so you can see how this process works. Once you have this knowledge, you can build on it to make entire plugins and even themes multilingual.

Translation Functions

Let's take a look at the first two built-in WordPress functions for translating UI strings. We can use: __() and _e().

__() Function

__()[2] is a double underscore followed by the function parentheses. The parameters to this function are the text that you need to translate and the domain (your plugin) where the translation connection can be found. The domain here relates to the use of the load_plugin_text_domain() function—more on that later. If WordPress locates the correct translation, then the new language text is returned. If there is no translation content found, then the original English text is returned. To change the displayed language in the admin area, select Settings > General > Site Language. We will look at this again when we test our translation efforts at the end of this chapter. Here is a code example for using the __() function:

```
$trans_text = __('Revenge is a dish best served cold','architect-subscribers');
```

---

[1] multiple languages: https://phpa.me/multilingual-wordpress
[2] __(): https://developer.wordpress.org/reference/functions/__/

You can then use the translated text in any area of your plugin you want using the contents of the `$trans_text` variable. The first function parameter can also be a variable. This option allows for more ease when building a complex or dynamic string that you want to translate:

```
$raw_text = 'Revenge is a dish best served cold ' . ' - do you agree?';
$trans_text = __($raw_text, 'architect-subscribers');
```

_e() Function

The next translation function is the "single underscore e" function, _e()[3]. Unlike the __() function, the translated text is echoed out to the browser immediately rather than returned to be assigned to a variable. Here is a code example:

```
$raw_text = 'Some text to be translated and displayed right away';
// echo this translation to the browser directly
_e($raw_text, 'architect-subscribers');
```

Other Translation Functions

There are other translation functions[4] you can make use of for individual cases.

The _n() function can be useful when displaying dynamic content that may have single or plural translation text depending on the context. An example of this would be describing how many books you may have. Here is a code snippet that returns a string showing the interpreted number and context of a phrase based on the singular or plural of what you are describing. The printf()[5] function replaces the %s placeholder with the $count value. This approach can be tricky with different languages, so be sure to test this in the language you intend to use.

```
$count = 1 ;
printf( _n( 'I have %s book', 'I have %s books', $count, 'text-domain' ),
        number_format_i18n( $count )       );
```

Also check out the esc_html__()[6] and the esc_html_e()[7] functions which escape any HTML before returning it or displaying it. Use these when you are outputting data that came from users. We can accomplish most of the additional translation functions with

---

[3] _e(): https://developer.wordpress.org/reference/functions/_e/
[4] translation functions: https://phpa.me/wp-plugins-intl
[5] printf(): https://php.net/printf
[6] esc_html__(): https://phpa.me/wpdev-eschtml-2
[7] esc_html_e(): https://phpa.me/wpdev-eschtml-e

native PHP functions, but it's straightforward to use the WordPress equivalents when possible.

Preparing Your Code

How do the translation functions know how to retrieve a translated string? The load_plugin_text_domain() function tells WordPress where to look for available language files. It has three parameters, one of which is deprecated, so you only need to be concerned with two of them.

The parameters are:

1. $domain—This is a unique string that tells WordPress what plugin will be using the language files. It connects all the other language functions that you will be using. For simplicity, use the same text here as the name of your plugin.
2. $abs_rel_path—Deprecated, simply set this value to false.
3. $plugin_rel_path—Relative path to all translation source files your plugin will be using. You could create a directory named languages/ in your plugin's root. In our sample plugin, it would be 'architect-subscribers/languages'.

This function should be defined in your main plugin file, so all aspects of your plugin can make use of the translation features even if they are not needed immediately. The location in that file for this function call is not all that important, but I place it just after I set my plugin defined constants so I can make use of the constants. Here is the code for pointing to the translation files:

```
/* ==================== */
/* Load language pointers */
/* ==================== */
function arch_subscribers_languages() {
    load_plugin_textdomain('architect-subscribers', false, 'architect-subscribers/languages');
}
add_action('plugins_loaded', 'arch_subscribers_languages');
```

You have to register the language inclusion with a call to the add_action() function that calls a function you create that, in turn, calls the load_plugin_text_domain() function. This is loaded according to the first parameter of the function, namely when the plugin is loaded.

Translating A Settings Page

Let's continue with the translation of our plugin's settings page to Italian. As shown in Figure 7.1, we have five different locations on the display that we want to translate. This (3) is the help text that displays when a user's pointer hovers over the question mark.

The first thing we need to do is find the location of these strings in our code. Then, we change their display method to use either the __() or the _e() functions depending on our situation and preferences.

The first place to change our code (1) is where it displays messages to our plugin users. The location of the code for (1) on our page is where we show messages to the user on success or failure of page submission. The original code in our architect-config-page.php code file is this.

Figure 7.1.

```
if (isset($_POST['submit'])) {
    check_form();
} else {
    $message = "Adjust settings to your preferences";
    show_form($message);
}
```

> *Keep in mind we are only setting the locations in our code where we want to translate content. The actual translated text does not exist yet; that comes later.*

Here we are testing to determine whether the page has been displayed or if it has been submitted. In the else condition, we set up the initial message to the user. Since we are not displaying anything directly, we use the __() function. The new code to load the $message variable looks like this:

```
$message = __("Adjust settings to your preferences", 'architect-subscribers');
```

The other location in our code where we load text into the $message variable is when the form is submitted, and we have to send out a confirmation or failure message. There are a few locations where this is done in the check_form() function. They are listed here and can be found if you follow along by searching for the $message variable. Here is the pre-altered code:

```
$message = "<b>" . "token prefix field cannot be blank." . "</b>";
```

and

```
$message = "Configuration Changes have been saved";
```

The updated code looks like this:

```
$message = "<b>" . __("token prefix field cannot be blank.", 'architect-subscribers') . "</b>";
```

and

```
$message = __("Configuration Changes have been saved", 'architect-subscribers');
```

In both cases, we simply interject the __() function where we want to insert the translation. The text for the submit button (3) follows a similar approach. Here is the pre-altered code:

```
submit_button("Save Settings", "", "submit", "" ,$btn_attributes);
```

The only difference is it creates more readable code to load the text into a variable and use that translated text in the submit button function. Like so:

```
$submit_text = __("Save Settings", 'architect-subscribers');
submit_button($submit_text, "", "submit", "", $btn_attributes);
```

On our screen (2) is the display of the form field labels. Again we need to see where they are being displayed in the code and use one of our translation functions.

Our original code looks like this:

```
<p style='display: inline; <?= ($label == "email_updates") ? "color:red" : ""; ?>' >Send Post Updates by email?</p>
```

Since we're already echoing the text to the browser, use the _e() function. This has to be done within the context of PHP/WordPress code; we have to alter the code a little more drastically than in our previous two situations. Here is the altered code:

```
<p style='display: inline; <?= ($label == "email_updates") ? "color:red" : "" ?>' >
<?php _e("Send Post Updates by eMail?", 'architect-subscribers') ; ?>
</p>
```

The approach for all the form labels is the same; wrap the text in PHP code and use _e() to echo the content.

The Loco Translate Plugin

Now that we prepared the code for translating content, we have to get the actual translation text and add it to our translation files. Thankfully, there is a plugin for that! Locate, install, and activate the "Loco Translate" plugin[8].

Once installed, you can see it on the admin menu. Clicking on the "Plugins" menu item (1) shows a page similar to that of Figure 7.2. This page lists all of the installed plugins. You can then select the one you want to create translations for. We need to choose the "Architect Subscribers" (2) plugin.

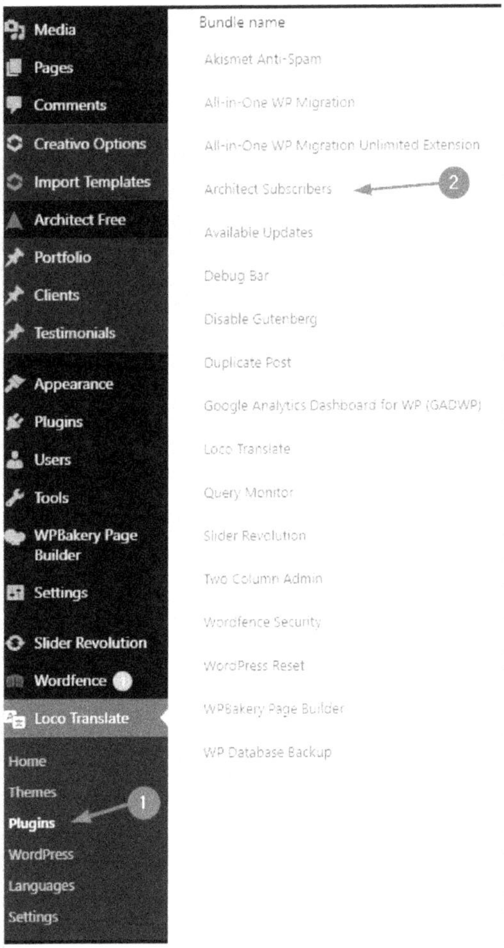

Figure 7.2.

[8] "Loco Translate" plugin:
https://wordpress.org/plugins/loco-translate/

Creating A Template File

Next, you should see a page like what is shown in Figure 7.3. Here there are two options, and because we are here for the first time, we have to create a template (1). A template is a basic scan of the selected plugin code for all of the translation options. Following this process creates a POT file[9] we can use to add more language translations. For now, we are scanning our code for the language functions we added above with the __() and _e() functions.

Figure 7.3.

Clicking on "Create template" shows a screen asking you to confirm the template's creation and location. You can set these options on the "Advanced" tab, including where you want the specific language translation files stored. Be sure to go to the Advanced tab and set the value for "Domain Path." If set to "languages," this setting allows you to save your language files in the same folder at your POT template file. After confirming the creation of the POT file, WordPress redirects you to the plugin overview screen, where you can now create

Figure 7.4.

a language set. Click (2) to create a new language. You should now be on the screen shown in Figure 7.4.

Performing The Translations

Select the language that you want to use (1)—we have selected Italian—and the location where you want the translation files to be stored (2). Keep in mind the chosen folder must be writable by WordPress to create the language file. This requirement also holds for the .pot file we created previously. Once you have confirmed your selected language and location, click the "Start Translating" button, and it scans your code for all available places setup for a translation. You should see a screen like the one shown in Figure 7.5.

---

[9] POT file: https://phpa.me/wpmake-pot-file

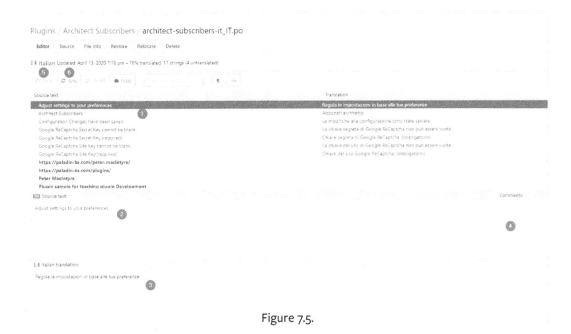

Figure 7.5.

We do the bulk of the translation work here. This (1) shows all of the text in your plugin marked as translatable. You can see some extra text items from the plugin header section where you identify the plugin name, author, version, description, and so on. You can ignore these if you want. We have already translated the first three items. You can see for the one being worked on, "Token Prefix:" that the source text is shown separately (2), and then area (3) is active where you would paste in the translated text. If you want to add any helpful comments, you can do so on an item-by-item process in the comments area (4). For simple translations, you could use Google translate and copy/paste the translations in. Save the translations as you go (5), and if there are any new phrases to translate over time, be sure to "sync" (6) the translation file you are working on with the master POT file. To return to the plugin level, click on the plugin name at the top of the page, where it is shown in a crumb bar fashion. Then, you can update your template file, if needed, and in turn, sync your language-specific files, as well.

Viewing The Results

Now all you have to do is test the translation by selecting your desired language (2) in the Settings > General (1) page and save your changes. Figure 7.6 shows this.

Check your page where the translations should appear. As you can see, in our case, the Italian shows where we wanted it to (see Figure 7.7).

Be sure to test these translations for accuracy. Frequently, a simple Google translation is not in the right context. Also, since you are altering your code, you should retest anything you have done from top to bottom.

Figure 7.6.

Figure 7.7.

Chapter

8

The Best Plugins—Part One (Simple Tasks)

There are a plethora of free plugins[1] available for WordPress. At the time of this writing, there are 56,777 active plugins available, not including the many that are commercially available. But—and this is a very big but—not all of these plugins are useful or applicable to a broad user audience. Some plugins are created and released into the wild. Then, their creators left them to wither on the vine, so to speak—never being updated, tweaked, maintained, improved, or worse: debugged.

---

[1] plugins: http://wordpress.org/plugins

8. The Best Plugins—Part One (Simple Tasks)

When you look at their details on the WordPress site, most plugins provide the information needed to make an informed decision on whether or not you should trust it enough to try it out or even use it long term on your site. See Figure 8.1, for an example of this on the information page of Akismet.

Figure 8.1.

First, vet that the plugin's intent aligns with what you want to accomplish on your site. Read the title and the description of the plugin, and maybe even look at the screenshots. You should take note of its compatibility with your installed version of WordPress.

The additional essential items to look for are:

- The date of the last time the plugin was updated. Keep in mind that a recent update date does not necessarily mean the plugin is great. An older age could mean a plugin has already gone through several updates, and the developers are happy that it is stable and, therefore, not in need of any further updates.
- The number of downloads; this is a raw measurement of the plugin's popularity and usefulness.
- An active "Support and Reviews" section. It implies proper attention from the developer to any reported issues and valuable feedback from the user base.

In concert with one another, these can lend credence to the plugin in question.

All these factors, however, do not guarantee a great plugin. Going through a vetting process for every plugin can be a tedious and overwhelming task. Therefore, we have selected many useful plugins for handling frequent tasks and website capabilities. We describe them in the next two chapters. This chapter covers what we describe as "short-snappers"—simple, usually one-task plugins almost every site can benefit from implementing. The following chapter covers more extensive multitask plugins like WooCommerce, the ecommerce plugin.

Full disclosure: We did not test all 56,000+ plugins! These are the plugins we use and have found to be stable, functional, and well supported. You may discover a similar plugin that suits your needs better.

Caution! You should be conservative in your plugin use. Employing many plugins can lead to higher overhead in demand for CPU and memory, potentially reducing site performance. Also, the more plugins you have, the more often you have to perform updates to keep your site secure and current.

How To Install And Activate A Plugin

There are several ways to install plugins on a WordPress site. In this section, we will be discussing the two most popular ones: seek + install and upload + install. You can perform both of these methods within the administration area. Another technique (not covered here) is to use FTP to upload files directly to your server and activate the plugin later, but that is only done in rare circumstances. We do not recommend the FTP approach unless you know what you are doing. FTP access is not always secure, and since it allows for direct access to the file base, it can also be prone to human error.

For simplicity, we are installing all of our plugins in the next two chapters with one of these two standard methods, primarily the seek + install method.

If you have any trouble with either of these methods, check this page for trouble-shooting tips[2].

The Admin "Seek + Install" Method

With this method of plugin installation, you access the Plugins > Add New menu item. Doing so brings up the "Add plugins page;" see Figure 8.2. You are initially shown some featured plugins. There are other menu items you can use to see what's popular,

Figure 8.2.

---

[2] troubleshooting tips: https://phpa.me/wordpress-troubleshooting

recommended, and on your list of previously marked favorites (if you have already done this on WordPress.org). These four menu options are nice to use if you're exploring, or you want to see what is trending in the WordPress community.

If you know what plugin you are after, and usually you do, type in the name or topic of the plugin in the "Search plugins" input field at the top right of this page and press **enter**. As you can guess, shopping for a plugin can potentially take hours. Once you find the plugin you're after, you can investigate it further by clicking the "more details" link. This opens a pop-up window giving you all the available details you might need. Typical detail tabs are description, installation, screenshots, change logs, FAQ, and reviews.

If you are sure this is the plugin that you want, click on the "Install Now" button to start the installation process. WordPress may ask for FTP credentials depending on how your site was initially installed. When completed, you are shown the "Activate" button. Click on that to make the plugin live. You are then redirected to the "Installed Plugins" page, which lists all plugins currently installed.

Once a plugin is activated, you should see some proof of this in the admin menu. Sometimes, the plugin inserts its own menu item. Other plugins, however, show up under the tools menu or the settings menu. There is no hard and fast rule here, so if you don't see a newly created top-level menu item for your plugin, you may have to hunt a little. Keep in mind that some plugins are additions to the core functionality of WordPress and, therefore, may not have a menu item presence at all. As a last resort, you can also look at the plugin in the list of installed plugins to see if there are links for settings and plugin support directly under the plugin name itself.

The "Upload + Install" Method

The other method, usually used with commercially available plugins, is to download a .zip file from another site and upload it via the Admin area. As an example here, we use the "All-in-one Migration" plugin. After locating the desired plugin on WordPress.org, or at the website hosting the plugin, download it to your local filesystem. Next, go to the same Plugins > Add New page in the admin area, and this time click on the "Upload Plugin" button at the top of the page. This presents you with a file browsing dialog. Locate the .zip file you downloaded, select it and then click the "Install Now" button shown in Figure 8.3.

All the remaining steps are the same as the previous method in that you have to activate the plugin and then locate it within the admin menu system to make use of it.

Figure 8.3.

Akismet

Akismet[3] is a strange name for a plugin; it's a default plugin on most WordPress installations, and there is a good reason for this. Most blog sites allow for comments to be appended to posts or pages by readers. Comments allow users to reply with their thoughts and ideas on the post or page topic. However, bots and malicious software engines can add spam to your posts. The spam these entities generate can quickly overload a site that does not do an adequate job of protecting itself. Even if you don't use this plugin, you should always have your comments set to "Pending" so you or someone else must review and approve any comments added to your blog before publishing them on your site. Under the Settings > Discussions menu option, be sure that you have "Comment must be manually approved" turned on. Be sure to review the other options available to you on this screen, as they may also help combat comment spam.

Getting back to the plugin in question, Akismet analyzes any incoming comment submission and flags spammy ones for review. Once you activate the plugin, it prompts you to provide an API key. The Akismet folks use this key for statistical purposes. Akismet is free for personal blogs, but they do offer a commercial version, as well.

> Actually, many plugins have a free version with some limitations, such as reduced features or reduced uses. Be sure to double-check the license requirements on each plugin you use to ensure that you are honoring their licensing requirements.

Once you have the API key in place, you have even more options available to you for handling spam. See Figure 8.4 for the available options.

You can always return to this settings page by way of the Settings > Akismet menu option.

Figure 8.4.

Available Updates

A plugin created by one of this book's authors is called Available Updates[4]. After using WordPress for many years and having many sites to manage and maintain there

---

[3]   Akismet: http://www.akismet.com
[4]   Available Updates: https://phpa.me/wp-available-updates

was a moderate pain-point in having to navigate to Plugins > Installed Plugins, and then clicking on the "Update Available" link at the top of the page. Since it is important for security and site stability to keep your plugins up-to-date, this can be a very repetitive task when maintaining many sites. This added a lot of unnecessary clicks, so this plugin was created. If there are plugins to be updated, it takes you to the list of available plugins directly after you log in to the admin area. Time saver indeed! It's a free plugin but open for donations. Figure 8.5 shows the information tab for this plugin.

Figure 8.5.

Testimonial Rotator

The Testimonial Rotator[5] plugin displays multiple quotes or testimonials in a compact and limited space. It typically shows content in a sidebar location via a widget. We can use it to draw attention to particular sections, pages, or to list testimonials from people who have sent you praise for your work or accomplishments.

After installation and activation, you should see a new menu item called "testimonials" at the admin menu's main level. Here you create rotators (you can have multiple rotators for different contexts of your site), enter the testimonials, and fine-tune behavior. You can set display time length, transition effect, the attached image's size, and the transition speed between testimonials. You can add the rotators directly into individual pages, as there is an "Add Rotator" button included in the text editor on both pages and posts.

Figure 8.6 shows the listing of existing quotes that have been entered with the option to add more.

In Figure 8.7, we are editing an existing quote; we have rearranged the default layout here so your screen may look different. In add/edit mode, you can:

Figure 8.6.

---

[5] "Testimonial Rotator": https://wordpress.org/plugins/testimonial-rotator/

- control important options like giving a star rating,
- attach the testimonial to different rotators (you must create these beforehand),
- assign an author (with the option to add a link to a URL)
- and attach an image to the testimonial.

These are just a few of the many options and controls at your disposal.

The widget area where you can deploy these rotator looks similar to that in Figure 8.8. Here, we can further configure how the rotator appears in our sidebar.

Figure 8.9 shows the widget in its deployed environment.

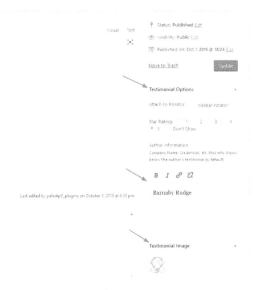

Figure 8.7.

Figure 8.8.

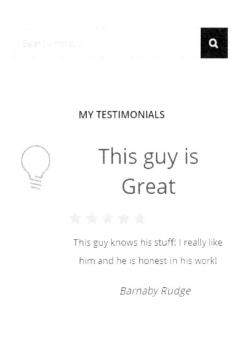

Figure 8.9.

Custom Sidebars

The Custom Sidebars[6] plugin is more niche but very useful if employed well. It allows for different sidebars to be designed and implemented for different locations within your website. For example, you may have a portion of your site dedicated to ecommerce and want some shopping cart widgets to only show up in that context. Doing so lets you and content editors manage what widgets appear in a sidebar through the WordPress UI instead of in template files.

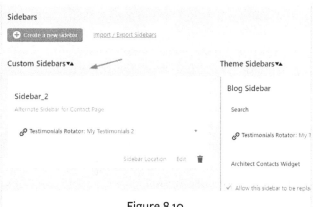

Figure 8.10.

In our example, we created two different pages and assigned each page their custom sidebar. This plugin takes over the widget area (again, no admin menu additions) and allows you to name and create sidebars. Figure 8.10 shows these sidebars and the widgets for each one. Sidebar_2 is the new one.

In Figure 8.11, you can see where it is assigned to the "Contact Us" page.

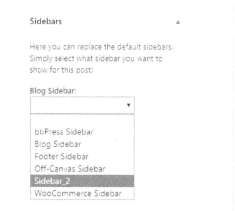

Figure 8.11.

Store Locator Plus

Store Locator Plus[7] is excellent for helping site visitors find your physical locations on a map. It is usually placed on a "Contact Us" or similar page; you can use it in multiple locations. This plugin integrates with Google Maps. For example, if your site is for a local community college, you could place a map locator for each building on campus. If your website was for a church, you could make locators for the locations of satellite Bible studies. The options and permutations are endless. Don't let the name fool you; if you aren't selling something, you can still use this plugin; it's not only for stores.

---

[6] Custom Sidebars: https://wordpress.org/plugins/custom-sidebars/
[7] Store Locator Plus: https://wordpress.org/plugins/store-locator-le/

After installing, activating, and getting a Google map API key (instructions are on the plugin Info Tab), you should see a top-level admin menu item named "Store Locator Plus." Here the "Plus" refers to their commercial version of this plugin. However, all the free version features should be more than enough to get you started. Begin by clicking on the locations option and select "Add." You are presented with a screen like that shown in Figure 8.12. Enter all the pertinent information and save it.

Next, you want to control how this information shows on the map and how the map itself is displayed. To do this, click on the "Settings" menu option and then the "Map" sub-menu tab, as shown in Figure 8.13. You can set the map's dimensions, the map type (satellite, roadmaps, etc.), the markers you want to use, and the map default location, language, and zoom levels. There are quite a few options here, so be sure to try them all until you get what you want.

Figure 8.14 shows the map location as added to the "Contact Us" page with Balmoral Castle in Scotland (the Queen of England's summer residence) as the starting point. You can use latlong.net[8] this website to help you with Latitude and Longitude values.

To use this locator on a page, add the shortcode [SLplus] to the text area and voila! You can use many extended attributes on this plugin, but they are mostly wrapped in another paid add-on plugin.

[8] latlong.net: https://www.latlong.net

Figure 8.12.

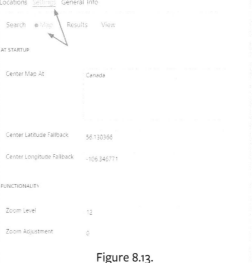

Figure 8.13.

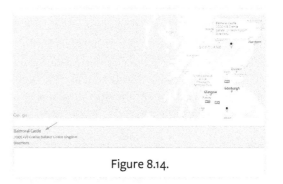

Figure 8.14.

Duplicate Post

The Duplicate Post[9] plugin can save you lots of time on page and post generation. If you have a page that is close to what you want, you can use this tool to duplicate the page so you can experiment with changes and not affect the original. It clones a page or post into a new draft and copies everything in the original. You can use it to copy a post and then change the content and maybe the featured image to quickly get new post content on to your site. After installation and activation, you should see a link on your post and page lists with "Clone" added to it. See Figure 8.15.

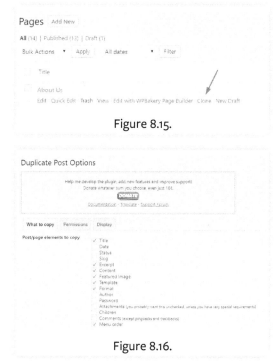

Figure 8.15.

Figure 8.16.

You can control the features of this plugin from the Settings>Duplicate Post menu path. Once there, you can control the elements you want to copy when you clone a post or page. Figure 8.16 shows some of the options available to you. This is one of the best content time savers you can add to your WordPress site.

Minimal Coming Soon & Maintenance Mode

Occasionally in the life of a website, you may need to temporarily disable the public interface while performing updates or layout changes in your admin area. You don't want your site visitors to see partially completed pages during this time, so you should make use of the Minimal Coming Soon & Maintenance Mode [10] plugin. After installation and activation, you should see a new entry on the top menu bar called

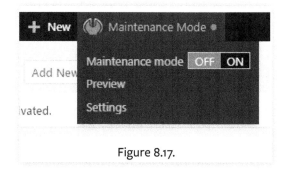

Figure 8.17.

[9] Duplicate Post: _https://wordpress.org/plugins/duplicate-post/_
[10] Minimal Coming Soon & Maintenance Mode :
    https://wordpress.org/plugins/minimal-coming-soon-maintenance-mode/

"Maintenance Mode" with a red dot beside it. If you hover over it, you should see a few options available to you (see Figure 8.17).

- A toggle to quickly switch your site to maintenance mode,
- a way to preview the site in its current state, and
- a link to the full list of plugin settings.

On the settings page, you can control what the site looks like and control the message to show your site visitors while it is in maintenance mode. Figure 8.18 shows a site in maintenance mode.

Figure 8.18.

Add From Server

Another great plugin to consider is Add From Server[11]. Frequently, web hosts limit the file size of media (and files in general) that can be uploaded. This plugin gets around files size limitations and assumes you have FTP upload access. This plugin does not circumvent any limitations on overall disk space quotas your hosting account may impose. After installing and activating the plugin, you should see "Add From Server" on the Settings menu. Clicking on the menu item brings up the options page for you to adjust as needed. See Figure 8.19 for a sample.

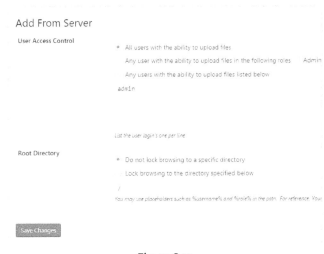

Figure 8.19.

You can restrict the user level that can perform large file uploads and where they can place files. Be sure to carefully consider who can use the plugin and what directories they can use.

Once you have your plugin configured, you can upload larger files via FTP and import them to your site's media library. A new menu item is also added under Media called "Add From Server." You can navigate to the folder that you have uploaded the large file to and

---

[11] *Add From Server: https://wordpress.org/plugins/add-from-server/*

import it into the media library. You can confirm this worked by navigating the Media files page where you should see the added files.

> Note: At the time of this writing, Add From Server had not been updated for two years, so use with caution.

Pop-up Maker

Next, we're looking at Popup Maker[12]. This plugin allows you to display interstitial pop-up messages on your site. Some designers and website visitors consider this kind of "interruption" annoying, so use sparingly. However, we included it here because there are use-cases for it. Imagine you want to conduct a survey, draw attention to your mailing list, or you have a special discount on a product in your online store. There are use-cases for this plugin, but don't be a pest with it.

Once you install and activate the plugin, you should see a new menu item added to the admin area called "Popup Maker." You can add multiple pop-ups and control when, where, and how they appear. Figure 8.20 shows a pop-up being created and some of its content and settings.

You can control the look and feel of your pop-ups, whether you have one or several. You can even create multiple pop-ups that look the same but have different content. Figure 8.21 shows the theme control page, which allows you to do this.

Figure 8.20.

Figure 8.21.

---

[12] "Popup Maker": https://wordpress.org/plugins/popup-maker/

There are many settings and controls that you use on your pop-ups. Perhaps you want to add a "never show again" control, change the CSS of the pop-up, add an image, change how the pop-up shows up and how it closes down (animations), or whether it appears on mobile devices, etc. These are all options. Be sure to test and make your pop-ups efficient and effective. Figure 8.22 is one example of a pop-up in action.

Figure 8.22.

Simple Links

The next plugin to consider is called Simple Links[13]. It provides a clean way to manage and display your site's links to other websites or web resources. If you have a research type of site, then this would be a great way to show your outside references or other websites related to your topic of interest.

After installing and activating the plugin, you should see a new menu item called "Simple Links." You can set broad settings in the "Settings" sub-menu and arrange the order in which they appear in the "Link Ordering" area. You can also manage your links by categories if you so desire (Link Categories sub-menu). Most importantly, you can add links with "Add New Links." The creation of a new link is shown in Figure 8.23.

Figure 8.23.

These links are then listed on a page you create. We called ours "Simple Links" and added it via shortcode like this:

```
[simple-links description="true" show_image = "true" remove_line_break="true"]
```

[13] Simple Links: https://wordpress.org/plugins/simple-links/

Figure 8.24.   Figure 8.25.

See Figure 8.24. You can control the display via options added to the shortcode. For example, you can do the following.

Change the sort order from ascending ASC (default) to descending DESC:

```
[simple-links description="true" order="ASC/DESC"]
```

Only show images.

```
[simple-links description="true" show_image_only="true"]
```

Limit the number of links to show.

```
[simple-links description="true" count="7"]
```

Navigate to the plugin's support page[14] for further details on the many shortcode options available.

Figure 8.25 shows the display of the links list on the public site. We can further tidy up the layout with custom CSS.

WP Super Cache And Autoptimize

Caching page output is one thing that can speed up your site. This is especially true if the page is not that data-dependent. Static pages like an about page rather than an often changing blog page, for example, can benefit. Cached pages download and display in a browser much faster. It can lead to more sales (if you are selling something on your site) as your potential customers do not lose interest and leave your site as quickly. Modern website

---

[14] *support page: https://onpointplugins.com/simple-links/*

visitors like their information fast and accurate; providing immediately displayed information keeps them happy.

> *Note: If you want to test your site speed, try out GTmetrix's tester page[15].*

Caching a page means storing most of the page's content in a static file or dedicated memory on the server. When a visitor requests a page, it's ready to go and can be downloaded immediately rather than waiting for WordPress to rebuild it.

WP Super Cache[16] can cache content. Figure 8.26 shows the settings for this plugin.

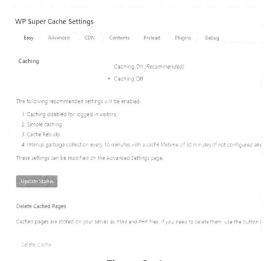

The primary setting is an on or off toggle for the plugin. However, you can delete the cached files at any time to force a reset of the cached files. Also, there are tabs with more in-depth options on them; Advanced, CDN, Contents, etc. On the "Advanced" tab, you can control the caching for certain site visitors, for pages using GET values, toggle the cache for mobile devices, and so on. In the CDN tab, you can control the content if you use a Content Delivery Network (CDN). It is a separate service to accelerate page delivery by offloading static files (images, CSS, JavaScript) to web servers closer on

Figure 8.26.

the network to your user. Do explore these options and be sure you understand them before changing anything, especially on a live site. The basic on/off status is all you need to get a significant reduction in page loading times.

Autoptimize[17] goes hand-in-hand with site caching. It optimizes your client-side content like JavaScript files, CSS, and images. All of these can take a long time to send to site visitors. "Minifying" the content of these files is one technique to make websites load faster. For text like JS and CSS, it reduces the file size by removing unnecessary characters before sending it to the client. These unnecessary characters include code comments, new line breaks, and extra white space. It's intriguing when you think about how much of this "filler" is in web files; it is all un-needed to serve a web page to a browser. The extraneous content is mostly

---

[15] *GTmetrix's tester page: https://gtmetrix.com*
[16] *WP Super Cache: https://wordpress.org/plugins/wp-super-cache/*
[17] *Autoptimize: https://wordpress.org/plugins/autoptimize/*

for human readability benefits, so stripping it all away can give you speed gains by reducing file sizes. On larger, more complex sites, this adds up over time.

Figure 8.27 shows the Autoptimize settings page found at Settings > Autoptimize. Here you can specify what aspects of your site you may want to optimize or minify.

Smush

Continuing with the topic of making your site load faster is the issue of managing images. Did you know that when you upload an image to the WordPress media library, you are actually creating at least three copies of the same image? WordPress does this behind the scenes for you, so your image is available in different sizes. On the client-side, this is beneficial. If you want to show a 150x150 image thumbnail on a page, you don't want to make your visitors download a large, full-resolution file. However, it increases how much disk space your site uses. If you don't manage it and if your site is heavy on images, you can run out of free disk space.

Figure 8.27.

Figure 8.28.

Smush[18] assists with image management by reducing JPG and PNG file sizes. It attempts to remove any unneeded metadata that can sometimes accompany a file without affecting the original image quality. It can also automatically resize images over a configured height or width. This metadata includes information like the latitude and longitude coordinates were an image was taken, information about the camera that took the picture, or the program used to create the image. Smush also has a bulk optimizing feature that runs over your already uploaded images, optimizes them, and intervenes with any newly uploaded files.

---

[18] Smush: https://wordpress.org/plugins/wp-smushit/

Figure 8.28 shows the Smush process underway on a sample website. Here (1) it tells you how many images it has found that could benefit from it. Then, when you start the Smush process, it shows you its total progress (2) and then the amount of space savings it is giving you (3).

WP Content Copy Protection & No Right Click

WP Content Copy Protection & No Right Click[19] is a plugin which may have limited use because it's for sites that want to try to protect their content to a degree. This plugin controls what can be seen or accessed when users click the right mouse button or attempt to copy-and-paste information from your website. A determined attacker won't have a hard time circumventing this, so if your information is highly confidential, then this is not the plugin for total content security. For that, you should use a membership style plugin, which only viewing content by authorized account holders.

If your content is that proprietary, then it should not be on the web at all!

If you want to prevent or at least hinder content harvesting from your site, use this plugin. It disables the pop-up menu you generally see when clicking the right mouse button. Figure 8.29 shows this typical menu as displayed in the Firefox browser.

Figure 8.29.

Note that there are two different menu pop-ups that display depending on the context. The first is displayed when no text is selected on a page—the other displays when there is highlighted text. Figure 8.30 shows the settings page for this plugin. It allows controlling what is displayed to your site visitors and can show a custom message if someone attempts to print-preview a page.

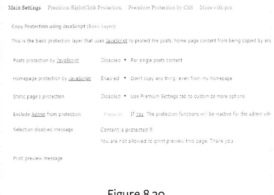

Figure 8.30.

[19] *WP Content Copy Protection & No Right Click:* *https://wordpress.org/plugins/wp-content-copy-protector/*

GDPR Cookie Consent

GDPR Cookie Consent[20] is likely more relevant to websites hosted in the EU, but all sites can benefit from the concepts the GDPR[21] (General Data Protection Regulation) proliferates and promotes. GDPR defines the data protection and privacy for all individual citizens of the European Union and the European Economic Area that must be in place and in force. Concerning websites and personal data, a general consent pop-up is often shown, stating that the site is in compliance with this law and that the visitor's data is safe. They also generally ask that a site visitor acknowledges this by clicking on an action button stating their agreement. More on the overall statements of this EU Law, go can be found on Wikipedia[22].

> *Note: If you have concerns over sites you manage and how they relate to GDPR, please consult your lawyer or legal counsel.*

As stated, regardless of where you host a website, GDPR compliance is still worth having on your site, as you may also have visitors from the EU. This compliance reassures them you are taking action to protect their, or anyone's, data. Of course, you should do more than just show a pop-up to a visitor. You should review all the guidelines of GDPR and ensure that what you are promising to a visitor to your site is in place and operational.

Figure 8.31 shows how the default settings affect the public side of your website.

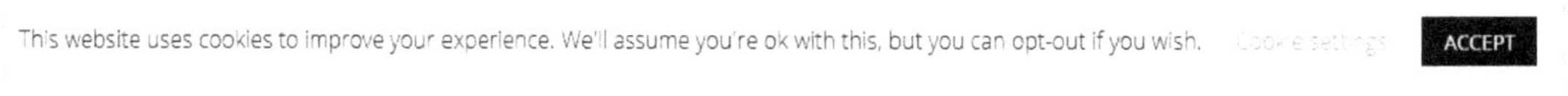

This website uses cookies to improve your experience. We'll assume you're ok with this, but you can opt-out if you wish.   Cookie settings   **ACCEPT**

Figure 8.31.

Figure 8.32 shows the options you can set. There are many options here, so be sure to explore them and try them out on a staging site before any live implementations. Remember, there can be significant legal implications if you are merely showing a consent pop-up and not following through with these guidelines.

Figure 8.32.

---

[20] *GDPR Cookie Consent:*
   https://wordpress.org/plugins/cookie-law-info/
[21] *GDPR: https://gdpr-info.eu/*
[22] *Wikipedia: http://phpa.me/wikip-gdpr-eu*

WP Rollback

WP Rollback[23] can save you time and potential headaches. From time to time, themes or plugins are released with minor, or even major, bugs. If a theme or plugin is distributed through WordPress.org[24] and you installed through the WordPress Admin area or directly downloaded it from WordPress.org, then you can mitigate the impact of said bugs.

This plugin makes available all the previous versions of any theme or plugin hosted by the WordPress system. In the event that you have a plugin that breaks or introduces a feature you don't like, you can roll it back to a previous version. Figure 8.33 shows the result of installing and activating the plugin. It adds a "Rollback" link to any of the installed plugins it finds that have been distributed by WordPress.org (1). If there is no record of the plugin found, then no link is added. The lack of an added link (2) means you likely have a commercial or "Pro" plugin installed.

If you want to switch to a specific version, click on the Rollback link, and you are offered a list of all releases that WP Rollback finds. Figure 8.34 shows this list for the Akismet plugin. Select the version number you are interested in and click the "Rollback" button at the bottom of the screen. There are some safety options here for you to consider, however.

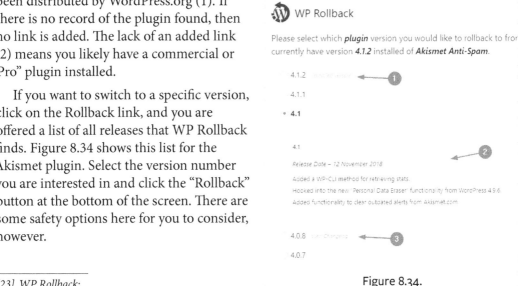

Figure 8.33.

Figure 8.34.

---

[23] WP Rollback:
`https://wordpress.org/plugins/wp-rollback/
[24] WordPress.org: https://wordpress.org/plugins/

First, you can see what current version you have installed (1). To see the change log, which lists the changes in a particular version, click on the "View Changelog" link next to a version (3) and that log displays (2). It's always a good idea to have your staging site or testing site to verify a rollback on your terms. Also, be sure to have a recent, working, complete backup of your site before making this type of alteration.

Custom Login

Another nice plugin to have on your site provides a custom admin login[25] page. If you maintain multiple sites, Custom Login provides a visual cue, a logo or image, to indicate you're on the right site. Generally, the logo of the site itself is used. There are also options to change the background colors of the login page and do things like turn off the screen shake when a login attempt fails. Figures 8.35 and 8.36 show how the simple image is changed on the login page.

The settings are found by going to Settings > Custom Login after the plugin is installed and activated.

Figure 8.35.   Figure 8.36.

[25] *custom admin login: https://wordpress.org/plugins/custom-login/*

Disable Gutenberg

So you weren't ready for Gutenberg, not many WordPress users were. Even though there was plenty of time to become familiar with it, some people simply do not like change. Enter Disable Gutenberg[26], which turns off the Gutenberg format and editor style for your pages and posts. If you are ready to make use of its new features, you can turn Gutenberg back on without much fuss.

Once installed and activated, you can navigate to the settings page by Settings > Disable Gutenberg. Here you see a screen like that shown in Figure 8.37. You have the option of turning Gutenberg off for the entire website (1), on a case by case basis (2), for user roles (Administrator, Editor, Author, etc.), or for post types (posts, pages, etc.).

Be sure to read our chapter on making the most of Gutenberg when you are ready for it!

Figure 8.37.

Wicked Folders

When it comes to organizing your posts and custom post types, categories, tags, and some custom taxonomies may not be sufficient. The ability to navigate quickly to the item you need to work on is crucial. For decades now, we've had the ability to browse via folders. This familiar UI is what this plugin brings to the WordPress' Admin—the possibility to organize your posts using folders, and to navigate a "tree of folders." By having that, you can interact with the UI in a more familiar manner, such as dragging elements and filtering by directories directly in the tree. The native alternative to this way of filtering on WordPress is to filter using the filters at the top of the posts/pages list. It is an alternative to existing functionalities that are not always as intuitive as an interactive folders tree.

The Wicked Folders plugin[27] has a free version and a pro version. The free version allows you to organize typical post types in folders. The pro version allows you to organize additional post types, such as attachments (media) and WooCommerce related post types such as products, orders, and coupons.

---

[26] "Disable Gutenberg": https://wordpress.org/plugins/disable-gutenberg/
[27] "Wicked Folders": https://wordpress.org/plugins/wicked-folders/

This plugin is frequently updated. However, their documentation doesn't mention available hooks; its customization might be for internal usage of the plugin's functionality only.

After installation, you can go to the admin page listing posts to see the folder's functionality. There, you can toggle the folder's panel, as shown in Figure 8.38.

You can drag posts to folders by clicking on the icon, as shown in Figure 8.39.

Certainly, this plugin offers one of the most intuitive ways of organizing posts on your WordPress site.

Figure 8.38.   Figure 8.39.

Force Login

While working with specific WordPress requirements for some clients, they may ask to place the site behind a "login wall." A login wall is when users must first sign in to access any page. It requires visitors to register an account, be approved, and potentially purchase a subscription or pay for access.

Many plugins accomplish similar functionalities. One recommended solution is Force Login[28]. When activated, it immediately hides your WordPress website behind a login wall. You can then use its hooks to whitelist the pages you want to allow access to. Force Login has been maintained for years and is updated according to the latest WordPress version.

To install and use it, you need to complete two steps:

1. Install the plugin
2. Activate it

---

[28] Force Login: https://wordpress.org/plugins/wp-force-login/

To customize it further via code, this plugin offers three filters: v_forcelogin_bypass, v_forcelogin_whitelist, and v_forcelogin_redirect. You can use these filters to bypass the login with custom programming of your own.

Figure 8.40. Force Login Plugin Page

At the v_forcelogin_bypass filter, you receive a Boolean value as a parameter and return a Boolean also. You can simply return a Boolean value according to what you want to do. In our example, we decided to keep returning the same variable with the changed value. If the returned Boolean is true, you are granted access; otherwise, access is denied. This is useful if you want to check for any condition that might affect this behavior, such as the time of the day or only allowing access to specific pages. In Listing 8.1, we allow access to particular pages and blocking access to everything else like pages/posts lists and the home page.

Listing 8.1.

```
1.  /**
2.   * Bypass Force Login to allow for exceptions. Here we are allowing access only
3.   * to single pages/posts.
4.   *
5.   * @param bool $bypass Whether to disable Force Login. Default false.
6.   * @return bool
7.   */
8.  function my_forcelogin_bypass($bypass)
9.  {
10.     if (is_single()) {
11.         $bypass = true;
12.     }
13.     return $bypass;
14. }
15.
16. add_filter('v_forcelogin_bypass', 'my_forcelogin_bypass');
```

The second filter, v_forcelogin_whitelist, passes an empty array as a parameter and expects an array in return. The URLs listed in the returning array are whitelisted. These URLs must be absolute, as shown in Listing 8.2.

8. The Best Plugins—Part One (Simple Tasks)

Listing 8.2.

```
1.  /**
2.   * Filter Force Login to allow exceptions for specific URLs.
3.   *
4.   * @param array $whitelist An array of URLs. Must be absolute.
5.   * @return array
6.   */
7.  function my_forcelogin_whitelist($whitelist)
8.  {
9.      $whitelist[] = home_url('/mypage/');
10.     $whitelist[] = home_url('/2019/03/post-title/');
11.     return $whitelist;
12. }
13.
14. add_filter('v_forcelogin_whitelist', 'my_forcelogin_whitelist');
```

The third filter (Listing 8.3), 'v_forcelogin_redirect', decides which URL this security layer redirects the visitor to. By using this filter, you receive the visited URL as a parameter, so you can choose where to redirect this visitor to by returning the destination URL. You may want to redirect users to a page where they can register or pay for an account.

Listing 8.3.

```
1.  <?php
2.  /**
3.   * Set the URL to redirect to on login.
4.   *
5.   * @return string URL to redirect to on login. Must be absolute.
6.   */
7.  function my_forcelogin_redirect()
8.  {
9.      return home_url('/register/');
10. }
11.
12. add_filter('v_forcelogin_redirect', 'my_forcelogin_redirect');
```

Another important consideration is that this plugin supports multi-sites when determining if the user is logged in and if the user has access to the requested sub-site.

Chapter

9

The Best Plugins—Part Two (Advanced Tasks)

This chapter focuses on plugins suitable for broader tasks. The plugins for more specialized tasks are covered in the <u>previous chapter</u>. This chapter deals with features that touch on ecommerce, search engine optimization (SEO), site protection, memberships, and Google Analytics, to name a few.

We can provide an introduction to using each, but you'll need to dedicate some time evaluating them on your own. You have to consider whether these plugins should be installed on your site as they generally take more admin area space (some even have a multi-menu system of their own). More importantly, they can also take some effort to set up and fine-tune beyond installation. If you decide to use any of these plugins, install them first on a testing site. That way, it doesn't matter if you make a mess while you learn—you won't be affecting a live environment.

Wordfence Security

The first line of the short description for Wordfence Security[1], from its creators sums up its purpose well:

> *"Wordfence includes an endpoint firewall and malware scanner that were built from the ground up to protect WordPress."*

It is a valuable plugin to have regardless of the subject matter of your site. Once you install and activate it, you can complete a series of set up steps, usually referred to as a "wizard." The plugin requests your email address to send you notifications from your site on any issues it discovers. Enter your email and click "Continue" to complete the initial set up. Figure 9.1 shows what this dialogue looks like.

Figure 9.1.

This plugin has many options related to site security and defense. To review those in detail, select Wordfence > All Options to get started. The top of this page is shown in Figure 9.2. Let's highlight the key features of this powerful plugin.

> *Once you have this plugin set up the way you want, be sure to use the export/import feature at the bottom of the options page to replicate these settings on other WordPress sites quickly. Doing so is a big time saver. It allows you to set the configuration on your testing site and then deploy those settings to your production site.*

---

[1] Wordfence Security: https://wordpress.org/plugins/wordfence

Figure 9.2.

> Note: Most of the options here have a small information icon—a question mark in a circle—linking to further descriptions and help about what a particular item is meant to accomplish. If you are not sure what a feature does, click this icon to open the Wordfence documentation site for more detail on the topic in question.

Be sure to explore the two categories of "Firewall Settings" and "Login Security." You can locate these option areas with the search box at the top of the options page. There are many firewall options; read them carefully to ensure that you have the settings you want. Settings available include:

- Whitelist and blacklist IP protections. These control who to let in and who to block from your site.
- Brute force defenses to mitigate automated attacks.
- Enforcement of strong passwords.

The Login Security category has its menu area—Wordfence > Login Security—it's that important! Be sure to access the "Settings" tab on this page to ensure you consider all the issues here like how many login attempt failures to forgive, how long to block someone who has failed to login, and if you want to enforce Two-factor authentication (2FA). You can also enable reCAPTCHA v3 on the admin login form if you wish.

On the Overall Options page, seriously consider enabling scheduled scans and automatically updating Wordfence. The first scans your site once every 24 hours (you get to choose the time of day if you are a premium customer). The second one updates the Wordfence plugin with updates as they are released—always a good idea to protect against newer vulnerabilities.

Under the email alert section, select the notification options you want. At a minimum, you should be notified when there are security breach attempts, and when plugins need attention.

Figure 9.3 shows a typical email that Wordfence generates. Here it is calling for its update. Depending on your notification settings, you could get many messages. Either set up a filter on your email system to automatically deal with email coming from Wordfence, or create a new email address specifically for this purpose. Whatever you do, don't ignore them.

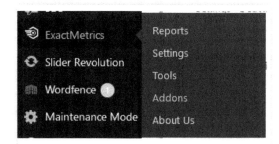

[Wordfence Alert] Problems found on milesinmyshoes.com

WordPress <wordpress@milesinmyshoes.com>
to me

This email was sent from your website "Miles in My Shoes" by the Wordfence plugin.

Wordfence found the following new issues on "Miles in My Shoes".

Alert generated at Wednesday 30th of October 2019 at 11:38:24 PM

See the details of these scan results on your site at: https://mailinmyshoes.com/wp-admin/admin.php?

Medium Severity Problems

* The Plugin "NextGEN Gallery" needs an upgrade (3.2.18 -> 3.2.19)

https://wordpress.org/plugins/nextgen-gallery/

NOTE: You are using the free version of Wordfence. Upgrade today.

- Receive real-time Firewall and Scan engine rule updates for protection as threats emerge
- Real-time IP Blacklist blocks the most malicious IPs from accessing your site
- Country blocking
- IP reputation monitoring
- Schedule scans to run more frequently and at optimal times
- Access to Premium Support
- Discounts for multi-year and multi-license purchases

Click here to upgrade to Wordfence Premium
https://www.wordfence.com/zz2-wordfence-signup/

No longer an administrator for this site? Click here to stop receiving security alerts

Figure 9.3.

Google Analytics Dashboard For WP

Google does a superb job of collecting site metrics. However, you have to go to the Google Analytics site to see the collected information. Google Analytics Dashboard for WP (GADWP)[2] connects to your Google account and presents the data within the Administration area of your WordPress site. ExactMetrics produce it, and you may see that name used in reference to this plugin, as well. The most recent version of this plugin moved some of the free features to the paid version; however, you still see valuable information with the free version.

Figure 9.4.

After you install and activate this plugin, you should see "ExactMetrics" added to the admin menu close to the bottom. Figure 9.4 shows it with its expanded sub-menu; note the name of the menu item is "ExactMetrics."

---

[2] *Google Analytics Dashboard for WP (GADWP)*: https://wordpress.org/plugins/google-analytics-dashboard-for-wp

During the installation process, you are presented with a setup wizard. Follow it's steps, which will ask you to grant access to the Google Analytics account for your website.

Figure 9.5.

Once the wizard completes, click on the ExactMetrics > Report menu item to load the main display area for your site's analytical display. Figure 9.5 shows this.

This summary report continues as you roll down the screen. The free version limits you to a rolling 30-day range of data. Some data points not visible in Figure 9.5 are "New vs. Returning" visitors, Device access breakdown (desktop, tablet, or mobile), Top 10 visiting countries, Top 10 referral sites, and Top Posts/Pages accessed. All of the other top-level menu items (Publishers, Search Console, etc.) are part of the Pro version. You can always see this data in your Analytics account. This plugin makes it available in WordPress, which helps the visibility of key metrics.

ExactMetrics adds itself to the Admin Dashboard submenu, but that link is another way to access the plugin's main reporting page. However, if you click on the dashboard menu, you can see a quick summary of the analytical data. This is shown in Figure 9.6.

This data can be helpful when looking at your overall site health and performance. Who visited your site from where and when, how long they stayed on your site, and what pages or posts they viewed are all useful data points. They help you specify and target your next marketing campaign, for example, and indicate what kind of content brings in new visitors.

Figure 9.6.

WP Forms

WP Forms[3] is used to create forms on your site so visitors can contact you. The paid version is not limited to contact forms. With WP Forms, you can create any form you can think of from a simple contact form, a much longer web survey, a work estimate quote form, and more.

---

[3]   WP Forms: https://wordpress.org/plugins/wpforms-lite

After you install and activate this plugin, the menu item labeled "WPForms" is added to the admin menu. Clicking on that menu item opens the listing of all existing forms if there are any. There are none on the initial installation. You can create as many new forms as you like by clicking "Add New" at the top of the page. Several basic form templates are available to speed up the form creation process when you want something simple. Form templates include a blank form, a simple contact form, a newsletter signup form, and a suggestion form.

Figure 9.7 shows the listing page with a single form.

Figure 9.8 shows an existing form in edit mode after selecting the "Simple Contact Form" template. You can add multiple styles of form fields to the form like drop-down lists, checkboxes, email fields, and reCAPTCHA protection. You can also designate some form fields as required.

Additionally, the integration with Google's reCAPTCHA[4] is easy to set up and adds another layer of spam protection from those annoying form-filling bots! On the WP Forms Settings (1) page shown in Figure 9.9, you can access the reCAPTCHA area via a tab by the same name at the top (2). Here you can choose the type of reCAPTCHA interface that you want to use. Once you provide the site (3) and secret keys (4)—from registering with reCAPTCHA—you should see the reCAPTCHA option on the form building interface for inclusion on your forms as desired.

Figure 9.7.

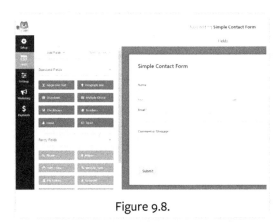

Figure 9.8.

---

[4] Google's reCAPTCHA: https://www.google.com/recaptcha/

You can also control any notifications or responses to send when a form is filled out and submitted. Click on the "Settings" tab and fill out the Notifications and Confirmations areas. Notifications let you know when a form is submitted. Confirmations send an acknowledgment email to the person who submitted a form to let them know you received it.

There are some other tabs on the left side of the interface where you can control the form settings and even control where to save submitted data. On the Marketing tab, you can integrate your form with a

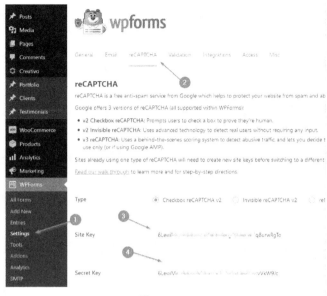

Figure 9.9.

supported email marketing platform like Constant Contact or MailChimp. In the Payments tab, you can integrate your form with a payment engine, but that feature is only available in WPForms Pro.

To display your form on a page, first look for the shortcode either on the right side of the listing of all your existing forms (WP Forms > All Forms) or on an individual form editor on the top right of the screen just to the left of the save button you should see the "</> EMBED" button. Clicking it displays the popup shown in Figure 9.10. Next, copy the shortcode or learn more about your embedding options by watching an instructional video. Placing the shortcode on your pages is the final step to having your forms active on your site.

Figure 9.10.

Revolution Slider ($)

Slider images or carousels are a standard design trend on websites. Although some may argue this design trend is on the wane, there are still many uses for an image slider that may not include a home page. You may want to show images from a recent conference that you attended or of a birthday party. There are many slider plugins available, but a versatile and user-friendly one we prefer is Revolution Slider[5]. It's a commercial plugin which you can also often find bundled with a commercial theme. We have it as part of the Creativo theme we frequently use.

Once you have installed this plugin, you should see a new menu item called "Slider Revolution" in the Admin menu. Clicking on it opens their specialized dashboard—a whole new design area that generally takes over the admin display. Here, you can work on existing sliders or create one from a pre-defined template or blank slate. There are over 160 templates you can use or purchase. Take some time to look at those for starting points. There are templates for religious use, marketing use, music/band use, ecommerce use, coffee shop use, news media use, and others. There are even post-based templates that automatically insert post images and excerpts to create a slideshow.

You may find a design that you like where all you need is to change some text and an image or two. The options within the slider are varied, so be sure to take the time to understand this product before you release your creations on the web. As we mentioned, this plugin comes as part of a theme bundle, and in our sample layout, we can include a slider for our home page. We will review that one here. Clicking on the pre-developed slider, we are taken to the design area, shown in Figure 9.11.

Figure 9.11.

---

[5] Revolution Slider: https://revolution.themepunch.com

There is much to unpack here. Let's touch on the surface points of interest. Area (1) is where you add element items to your slider—things like action buttons, images, or text. In (2), you can control what the overall slider looks like across different devices. You can have a different layout and design of the same slide deck on mobile devices than for desktop or tablet layouts. This flexibility is quite a nice feature! You can fine-tune the layer in focus (3) by setting the background color or hover color of a button, or the font size of the text. Area (4) controls the appearance style of each layer. For example, you may want to show text on the slider before you show a call-to-action button, and that button may slide in from the left of the display. All this can be controlled here and much more. As you can see, there are a lot of options and features here. Try not to get overwhelmed.

To display the finished slider on your website, expand the slider item (1) in the "Revolution" dashboard. After you save it, click on **Embed Item** (2) (Figure 9.12) to show the list of options available.

Typically, you use a shortcode in a text area to add a slider to a page. However, Figure 9.13 shows all of the possible ways to employ your slider.

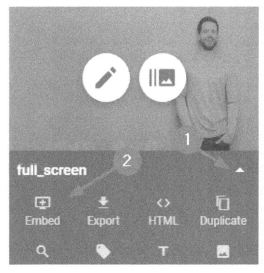

Figure 9.12.

Figure 9.13.

WooCommerce

Do you want to sell anything via your WordPress site? There are some excellent free ecommerce plugins available, and there are some great commercial plugins. Because we are trying to build our WordPress sites with free plugins when we can, we prefer WooCommerce[6]. It's a large and involved plugin that handles the many nuances of selling things

[6]   WooCommerce: https://wordpress.org/plugins/woocommerce

online. You can sell physical items like T-shirts or virtual items like training videos. You can manage inventory, control sale items, and duration, offer one-time discount codes, and manage how financial transactions are processed.

Locate, install, and activate WooCommerce. You may be given the option of walking through a setup wizard, which is valuable for first-time users. The wizard is helpful because it sets up your shopping cart, online shop, check out process, and account pages—for managing the information of returning customers. This alone is a great time-saver, so we recommended that you step through this wizard. Other steps in the wizard help you set up your store location to select a currency for you, set up your shipping and taxes, and set up your payment methods like PayPal, bank transfers, and checks.

Once installed, you should see a few menu items added to the admin menu, WooCommerce, and Products (refer to Figure 9.14).

First, add a product to your inventory by selecting Products > Add Product. The top portion of this interface should look familiar as it closely resembles the creation of a page or post. You should also see an area called Product Data; this may be further down the

Figure 9.14.

page. We have moved it up on our display so you can see it all in one image. Look at Figure 9.15 to see the entry of our sample product called "Widget 11" (1). We have provided a description (2). You must identify whether the product is a physical item that is shipped or virtual (like a web video or PDF) (3). You should also indicate pricing (4) for the product.

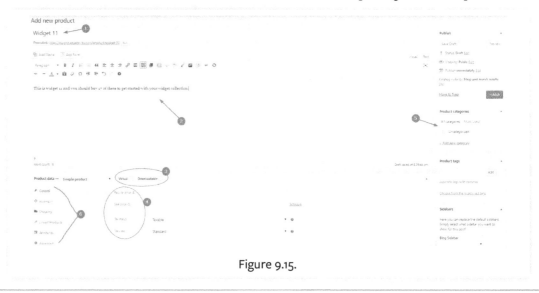

Figure 9.15.

Besides naming the product, you can also put it into a category (5) that you create and maintain. Doing so helps organize your online store if you have a large inventory. You can direct WooCommerce to handle and organize these categories as well. Under the Product Data section, you can see horizontal tabs (6) where you can further manage your product details. If you select the "Inventory" tab, you can control the product thresholds (stock on hand, and allowance for back-ordering) if it is a physical item. The shipping tab allows you to set the product's weight for calculating shipping fees; linked products enable you to upsell ("This other product has a better warranty") or cross-sell ("People that bought this item also bought this item").

Additionally, you should add a product image and decide if you want to allow user/customer feedback on your products. You can find these options on the individual product creation page.

You need to add these new pages to your menu system so your site visitors can see what you have on offer. We have added two widgets to the products list and added the "Shop" and "Cart" pages to the site menu. Figure 9.16 shows the Shop page and Figure 9.17 shows the Cart page.

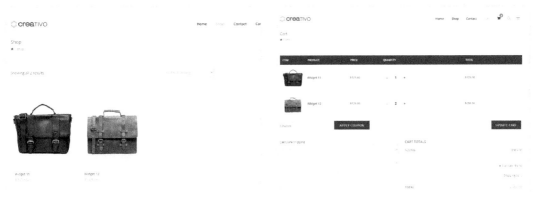

Figure 9.16.   Figure 9.17.

You can alter the colors of the action buttons and the other colors of WooCommerce with CSS if you don't like the default colors. Altering the CSS is generally done with your theme's CSS files. Often, this requires some iteration until you get the setting adjusted exactly the way you want. See our chapter on writing CSS and on Child Themes.

There are other pages and features you can set up and show within WooCommerce, such as allowing your customers to open accounts to save their addresses for future purchases, and so on.

To receive money from your customers, you need a connection to a financial service like PayPal, Stripe, BACS (direct wire transfers), or another payment processing gateway[7]. WooCommerce supports direct bank transfer and PayPal for simple transactions; plugins to handle other payment gateways need to be purchased, installed, and configured. PayPal Standard is sufficient to get started in ecommerce. It comes with a basic financial transaction processing and payment gateway system with a credit card payment alternative if needed.

When properly set up, it takes customers to a PayPal hosted page, which allows a customer to pay with PayPal funds or credit card. As a result, your site does not handle credit card numbers, which requires PCI compliance mandated by credit card companies. To see where to set up the financial integration, go to WooCommerce > Settings > Payments (tab), and then enable it under the Payments tab. Once enabled, click the manage button for that payment gateway to redirect to a screen where you can control the detailed settings. Figure 9.18 shows this settings page for PayPal.

Figure 9.18.

Notice here that you have to enable PayPal Standard, or you can alternately activate their "Sandbox" testing account. The sandbox feature is useful with a developer account. It allows you to test all aspects of Paypal integration without moving real money around while you build and fine-tune your ecommerce site.

WooCommerce comes with many additional add-ons to consider. You may want to use a different financial conduit like Stripe, have a UPS or FedEx shipping option to offer your customers, and so on. If you click on WooCommerce > Extensions, you can see a summary of the more common extensions you may want to implement. Keep in mind that many of these are paid extensions; be sure you will get your ROI (return on investment). WooCommerce's site has a list of all currently available extensions[8].

WooCommerce is a versatile plugin, and we can't cover every usage scenario it is capable of handling. However, we can highlight a few more key features. Be sure to explore the coupons area, the reports, and the shipping setup if you are dealing with physical products.

In the coupons area, you can create and manage discounts for your customers. You can have discounts for an entire purchase of anything in the shopping cart, fixed-rate discounts on individual items, or a percentage discount on select products. You can even set a coupon to have free shipping and set an expiration date for a coupon offer.

In the shipping area (Settings > Shipping), you can create and manage shipping costs based on local or national coverage regions.

In the reports section of WooCommerce, you can review detailed reports on all the activity of your sales efforts. Reports on three major categories are available—namely orders, customers, and stock levels. Within each of those three categories, you can dig deeper and get more detailed reports. For example, in the orders area, you can see how many orders were placed over a date range, how many coupons were redeemed, or how many virtual products were downloaded.

WooCommerce also adds a summary area to the WordPress Dashboard that provides a quick overview of your current ecommerce transactions. This is shown in Figure 9.19. Here you are shown a summary of your orders and any stock level warnings that may need your attention.

Figure 9.19.

Yoast SEO

Search engine optimization (SEO) is a science in and of itself. SEO is a collection of techniques to help your content rank and show up higher in search engine results. The struggle to get your site to the top of the Google search "food chain" takes careful thought, sound marketing, experimentation, and good luck. Either way, it's a good thing to attempt to get your site to the top of the search list so people can more easily find you when searching for your website's subject matter.

The Yoast SEO plugin[9] helps you target your SEO content on a granular level. You can evaluate the SEO content per-page or per-post, and the plugin offers helpful tips along the way.

> NOTE: Take a look at this Google guide[10] if you are entirely new to SEO concepts. Yoast has its own guide[11]. Learning more on this topic helps make your sites better and easier for your potential visitors to find. Read these and do some of your research online, as well.

---

[9]   Yoast SEO plugin: https://wordpress.org/plugins/wordpress-seo
[10] Google guide: https://phpa.me/google-seo-starter
[11] guide: https://yoast.com/wordpress-seo

Once installed, you should see a new menu item on the admin menu called "SEO." If you click on SEO > General after your install finishes, you can see helpful tips and any major SEO issues on your site currently. Figure 9.20 shows an example of this.

To configure SEO settings on a site-wide basis, you should start on the "Search Appearance" menu under the main SEO menu item. Here you add generic content about your site like its name and whether your website is for personal or commercial use. This is a general settings area that helps Yoast organize how your results display on search engines. There are other tabs here: Content Types, Media, Taxonomies, Archives, Breadcrumbs, and RSS. Explore these tabs to see how much there is to control on SEO at the site-wide level.

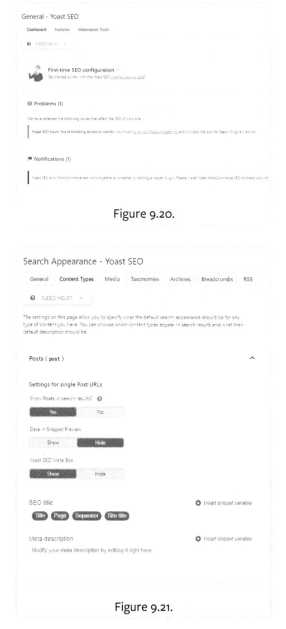

Figure 9.20.

On the "Content Types" tab, for example, you can control how your posts look on search results, and you can customize them from the default appearance. You can also give your content types a generic meta description. This is the least you should do for SEO. In the meta descriptions area for Content Types (SEO > Search Appearance > Content Types), one should try being more generic than specific. The descriptive text should be written with a site-wide perspective and not focus on any individual page. Choose your words carefully and be concise; this content may appear on your homepage and content type pages and is collected by search engines when they index your site. This is the first real step in getting your site higher on search result lists. Figure 9.21 shows the Search Appearance page with the "Content Type" tab in view.

Figure 9.21.

The time-consuming part is tailoring SEO content on individual pages and posts, but that's also where this plugin shines. Of course, your SEO results should improve if you add unique content to particular items on your site, but that does take time, effort, and creative skill. The trade-off here is having some SEO content for your site to at least participate in the search results game.

If you edit any page (we are looking at our "Sample Page" here), you should see a new section called "Yoast SEO." You can add your SEO content specifically targeted to the content of this page, as shown in Figure 9.22.

Once you add content and pick one or more keywords, the Yoast SEO plugin analyzes what you have entered. It offers recommendations under the "SEO analysis" section lower on the screen. Looking at Figure 9.23, you can see some problems reported on the sample content and a few positive items of note. Also note, when you add a meta description, the plugin builds a "Snippet Preview." This area shows how the page may appear on a Google search result. You can see just how important your SEO content can be. All of these SEO feedback can help to make your site more prominent on the web, so be sure to use this plugin to its full potential.

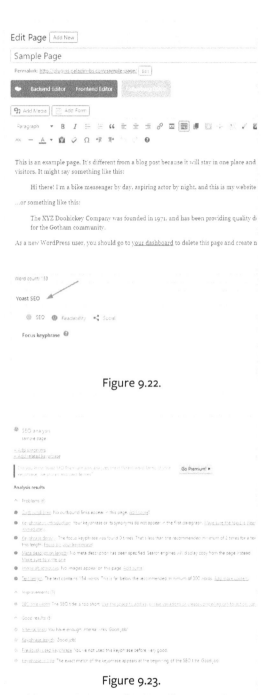

Figure 9.22.

Figure 9.23.

Ultimate Member

Ultimate Member[12] lets you control the content on your website and offer different levels of access, such as free versus paid (or multiple levels). Once you install and activate this plugin, you should see a notice at the top of the plugin page asking for permission to create the needed membership management pages, see Figure 9.24. You should allow this so the plugin can operate properly. Also, it saves you time as opposed to creating these pages yourself.

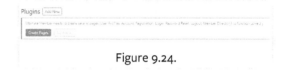

Figure 9.24.

Ultimate Member is added to your admin menu. Click on Ultimate Member > Dashboard to see a summary of the current memberships. This may not be very useful at the initial installation, but this information should be helpful over time. If you look at Ultimate Member > Settings you can find tabs where you can set:

- messages for unauthorized visitors to restricted areas,
- the outgoing email to new/renewing members,
- control the overall appearance of the membership areas, and more.

This plugin only controls access to restricted content as on or off, although you can override access on a per-post or per-page basis. There is no way to restrict access by custom post type such that different content is available based on membership levels.

Figure 9.25 shows that you can now control access to that item with a toggle on an individual page. By marking the checkbox, you are telling WordPress that only signed-in members can access this content.

Figure 9.25.

This is a rather straightforward plugin, yet it's quite powerful for controlling access to certain areas of your website. Be sure to explore all the settings this plugin offers to see how you can fine-tune all the membership aspects of a website. For example, on the Settings page and the Email tab, you can control all the outgoing email messaging generated by this plugin: account welcome emails, account rejected email, account deleted email, and password changed email. Also, on the Access tab, you can set the access level for the overall site to being restricted or not—instead of limiting access on a page-by-page basis.

[12] *Ultimate Member:* <https://wordpress.org/plugins/ultimate-member>

All-in-One WP Migration

All-in-One WP Migration[13] can save you buckets of time and headache. Its main feature facilitates the complete transfer of a WordPress site from one host to another—including all database information. After installation, you see a menu item added to the admin menu called "All-in-One WP Migration." You have three options: Export, Import, and Backups. We are looking at the free version, but you should consider one of the commercial versions. They remove file size limitations and—depending on the paid version you select (there are many)—you can automatically export to a cloud platform like Google Drive, Amazon S3, Dropbox, OneDrive, and others. Figure 9.26 shows the full list of export location options. Only the "File" option is available in the free version even though all the other destination options are shown.

As mentioned, this plugin is designed for migrating sites from one host to another. It does this very well and accomplishes it in two steps. The first step creates a full site and database backup that can be downloaded or exported to those cloud platforms mentioned. The second step requires installing this plugin on the target WordPress site and then restoring the backup file from the source server. You can upload the file with the Import menu option, but your web host or PHP settings may impose a maximum file size for upload files. You're likely to run into these limits with large databases or sites that use media files heavily. Here is where the pro version comes into play by removing file size limitations for backing up and importing the backed up files on another host. With the pro version, once you have the file uploaded to a folder path, it appears on

Figure 9.26.

---

[13] All-in-One WP Migration: https://wordpress.org/plugins/all-in-one-wp-migration

Figure 9.27.

the list of restorable backups. Figure 9.27 shows this interface with options on the far right of Download, Restore, or Delete. You can have multiple backups listed here.

If you want to restore a site based on one of the backup files, simply click the restore option on the same line as the desired backup file. After a warning that your entire site will be replaced (be careful), the plugin goes through the contents of the backup file and replaces all site designations like full URL paths with the target URL, if you are restoring a backup from a different URL. It also completely replaces the database content and structure. After the restoration is complete, you must sign out and sign back in to refresh your permalink settings. For security and space considerations, it is also good to remove any backup files from the list of backups after you are done using them.

This plugin, as per its name, is meant to be a migration tool. This it does very well. However, it should also be considered as an excellent site backup tool. Periodically create and download snapshots from step one, and you have a full site backup.

HyperDB

One of the main concerns for WordPress site owners is performance. WordPress' architecture might have many different bottlenecks depending on the plugins you have installed, your theme, server configuration, and database server. The HyperDB[14] plugin addresses database performance.

There is one concern about its functionality, though: You have to be able to configure your database instances or have someone who can do that for you. Replicating database instances and managing server configurations, might not be a trivial task or something your hosting provider allows. Having this option available can save much trouble when it comes to performance. Usually, this is a critical problem for businesses, which is why this plugin is on this list. If your site performance is not acceptable, it may be time to upgrade your hosting plan or find a new server provider.

Among its solutions, the most important ones are:

1. WordPress Multisite support. WordPress Multisite is a feature that uses one single instance of WordPress to serve multiple websites. Each site can have its own theme,

---

[14] HyperDB: https://wordpress.org/plugins/hyperdb/

set of active plugins, and its own domain. It requires extra data and database tables. Given this condition, this plugin becomes an essential option for performance improvement due to the third item.

2. Read and Write server replication. This solution allows you to have different servers for your database processes. You can choose to execute any write queries on one server and perform any read queries on another to balance your database layer's workload. More so, you can optimize the read server's settings to speed up SELECT queries, which tend to be the majority of queries. Slower queries that need to INSERT or UPDATE data won't impact overall site performance.

3. Different tables on different databases/hosts. Doing so can help some, especially for multisite WordPress instances where different websites are separated into different tables. That being said, you can distribute the various websites in your multisite environment across different database instances (located in different servers), spreading the load and improving the performance of all of the sites. This way, having one popular site experience a spike in traffic doesn't affect all sites.

4. Failover for a downed host. This option gives the website owner control of what to do when a failed connection to a database happens. Usually, WordPress displays an error on the screen. With this plugin installed, and after setting up read or write replication for your database, you can point the connection to try another working instance of the database.

Adminimize

One concern you might have when managing a website with multiple content writers is: How can I guarantee the users only have access to what they need? With too much information on the screen, the menu might be bloated with information that is not useful for that user's responsibilities, or even things the user shouldn't have access to. Adminimize[15] handles this tricky situation for you and customizes WordPress on the admin side.

Figure 9.28.

The administrative aspects of WordPress you can customize, per user role, include:

- which items users see in the Admin sidebar,
- if the Admin bar is visible in the frontend,

---

[15] Adminimize: https://wordpress.org/plugins/adminimize/

- which widgets are available, and
- which options are editable by users when editing posts and pages.

With Adminimize, you can control almost every one of these administrative aspects. You can deactivate everything from fields to menus, so you can be sure users only have access to what they need.

After installation, visit the following menu to customize access with Adminize (Figure 9.29).

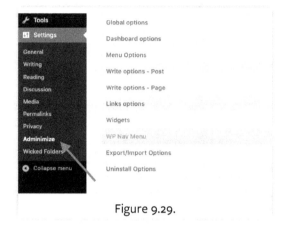

Figure 9.29.

Custom Post Types

Posts and pages are not always the only records that the user needs to display on their websites. We may need a custom way for users to store and manage the data they work with.

One example is how WooCommerce creates its products within WordPress: It creates a Custom Post Type called "product." They do that to provide a consistent set of fields for managing product records and keeping that separate from blog posts and webpages. If they were using common posts to register products, it would cause conflicts with existing websites that worked as a blog previously, as an example.

All site content data in WordPress is associated with a post and its metadata. By default, media (uploaded images and videos), pages, and posts are stored in the posts table. That is the core of WordPress flexibility. When a new type of data is needed, Custom Post Types[16] (CPT) is a great solution if you are not creating a very specialized functionality with unique requirements such as high performance. Even when it comes to that, we have alternatives to enhance the posts table's performance without moving away from it.

Included in CPT's benefits is the CRUD (Create Read Update Delete) procedure via the familiar WordPress UI, the navigation structure inherited from WordPress core, the set of permissions, default metadata, categories, tags; this list could go on and on.

Even though it is very flexible and part of WordPress' core, creating custom post types is not a trivial task, and it doesn't come with a UI. For that, you need to write custom code. This is where the CPT plugin comes to your rescue. You don't need to write code from scratch to create and manage custom data. You might need to go over some code to implement it in the UI or add some custom behavior when required. However, that's not needed

---

[16] *Custom Post Types: https://wordpress.org/plugins/custom-post-types/*

for basic behaviors like website presentation, listing, and searchability.

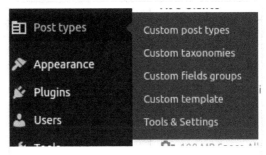

Figure 9.30.

Here is how to use this plugin. In Figure 9.30, we see the menu after activating the plugin.

The name of each option describes its purpose. The last option is about donating to the plugin creators or further documentation and support.

Figure 9.31 shows the form for Custom Post Type creation. In this form, we are creating a Custom Post Type called "Book."

The ID sets the actual post type slug name. This slug serves to identify this type of post. You'll see this in a moment when you list posts by their post type in the WordPress UI.

For example, this filtering might look like this depending on your settings:
`https://example.com/?post_type=book` or `https://my-website.com/book`.

The second item is the single name, used for presentation when you are administering it. As you can see in Figure 9.31, the left menu shows that name, "Book."

Notice that this is the "Simple View," and at the bottom of the Figure 9.31 we have the option for the "Advanced View," which displays the rest of the customizable options for names that might be shown throughout the application, here is the list:

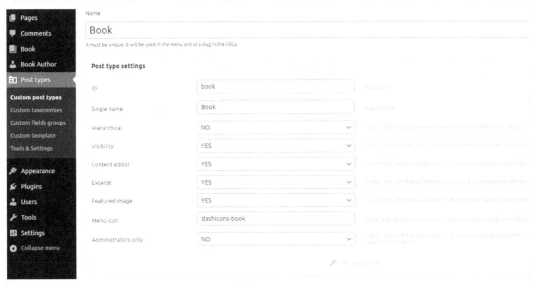

Figure 9.31.

- Add new
- Add new item
- Edit item
- New item
- View item
- View items
- Search items
- Not found
- Not found in trash
- Parent item
- All items
- Archives
- Attributes
- Insert into item
- Uploaded to this item
- Featured image
- Set featured image
- Remove featured image
- Use featured image
- Menu name
- Name admin bar
- Item published
- Item published privately
- Item reverted to draft
- Item scheduled
- Item updated

Each item in this list is explained in the form itself at the right. If not customized, WordPress uses a generic description. The more complex functionalities, which are Hierarchical and Content Editor, merit further explanation.

The Hierarchical option allows posts to have other posts as parents, like the default Page type. Pages can have "parent pages," which lets you structure their navigation like a folder or tree.

The core post is non-hierarchical and has a flat navigation.

The Content Editor option defines what editor is used when creating or modifying that post type's data. If you are using Gutenberg, the system automatically changes and uses the classic editor without the Content Editor for that post type, making available the default WordPress content editing, as shown in Figure 9.32.

Figure 9.32.

Posts 2 Posts

Posts 2 Posts[17] offers a complete development API for implementing relationships between posts.

Posts 2 Posts

By scribu

Figure 9.33.

[17] Posts 2 Posts: https://wordpress.org/plugins/posts-to-posts/

Some businesses need to relate information to keep data consistent with how it works outside of WordPress. You might have custom post types called books, and another post type called book-authors. It might be easy to maintain the relationship between books and their authors when you only have a few. You can manually update those posts, and keep them organized and related without much effort.

Having that manual organization might work with a few records, but it quickly becomes a nightmare as the number of records grows or when you have more people working in the system. Using this plugin, you can relate a CPT Authors with a CPT for Books. You can then quickly implement filters for searches, relate one-to-many, many-to-many, one-to-one, and generate reports. There is no limit to the possible logic you can build.

You can also develop plugins that, given the relationship, increase information consistency, and reduce the amount of maintenance needed when updating data or enhance functionalities that depend on the related records. To understand more, visit the plugin documentation[18].

After installing the plugin, you have to implement the relationship you need it to work with.

Let's think about some business requirements to see one example: Imagine your business needs to display a group of books for each author. To accomplish that, we can create CPTs; one for book records, and another for author records. While adding a book, the user should be able to select the authors related to that book. The other side should also be possible—to choose books when editing an author record.

You may be tempted to try it out with the existing "post types" that come out-of-the-box with WordPress: posts and pages. Our example uses two new post types instead, to show a real use case for this plugin's functionality. For that, we require the following post types: "Book Author" and "Book." We call it "Book Author," not just "Author," because WordPress already has an "Author" type, which is a post's author. Using the same name could cause conflict in the system.

To create those post types, we use the CPT plugin mentioned previously in this chapter. Using this plugin, we can create post types with the corresponding IDs: bookauthor and book. These IDs must be added as the IDs when creating the relationship in the next step; any typo can break this functionality.

The next step is to create a directory in your wp-content/plugins folder called my-relationship-plugin. Inside of it, you create a file called my-relationship-plugin.php. Add the code shown in Listing 9.1 to the file.

[18] plugin documentation: *https://github.com/scribu/wp-posts-to-posts/wiki*

Listing 9.1.

```php
1.  <?php
2.
3.  /**
4.   * Plugin Name: My Relationship Plugin
5.   * Plugin URI:  https://my-relationship-plugin.com/
6.   * Description: This is a sample relationship plugin.
7.   * Version:     1
8.   * Author:      WP in Depth Authors
9.   * License:     GPL v2 or later
10.  * License URI: https://www.gnu.org/licenses/gpl-2.0.html
11.  * Text Domain: my-relationship-plugin
12.  * Domain Path: /languages
13.  */
14.
15. function my_connection_types()
16. {
17.     'name' => 'bookauthor_to_author',
18.     'from' => 'bookauthor',
19.     'to' => 'book'
20. }
21.
22. add_action('p2p_init', 'my_connection_types');
```

Notice that the name attribute is a name you use further to refer to which relationship you are searching for. The from is the ID of one post type, and the to is the ID of the target post type. This relationship can have way more metadata and other conditions, but we are keeping it simple for basic usage.

This code adds a relationship between Book Authors and Books. By activating this plugin, you should see what is shown in Figure 34.

Navigate to Tools > Connection Types to see the connection you just registered, as shown in Figure 9.35.

You can now visit any post editor to see the options allowed by this relationship (Figure 9.36).

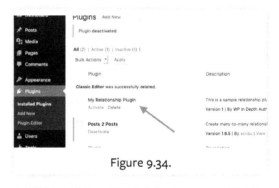

Figure 9.34.

Figure 9.35.

In Figure 9.36, there are three items you should take note of:

1. The new sidebar added by the new relationship.
2. The page added to the current post.
3. The space to search for more pages to relate to the current post.

You now have an advanced set of tools to implement advanced functionalities based on post's relationships.

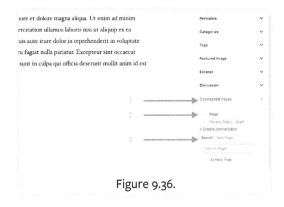

Figure 9.36.

With Post 2 Post, it's easier to implement features such as searching and filtering posts via their relationships. For example, on an author's page, we could list all of the books they've written. To accomplish that, we can proceed with two more steps:

1. Add a child theme, and
2. customize the single post page to list the relations we want to show.

We cover the procedures to create the child theme in Chapter 6. Here we assume that you are working in a child theme to customize your theme. You can also identify the theme's template hierarchy to select which file you need to customize in the next step.

At the page responsible for presenting a single-post, it might be something like `single-book.php` or `single-bookauthor.php`, (according to the theme's template hierarchy), place the code from Listing 9.2.

Listing 9.2.

```php
1. <?php
2. $queried_object = get_queried_object();
3. $watched_post_types = ['bookauthor', 'book'];
4. $is_watched_post_type = in_array($queried_object->post_type, $watched_post_types);
5.
6. if ($is_watched_post_type) {
7.     $connected = new WP_Query([
8.         'connected_type' => 'bookauthor_to_author',
9.         'connected_items' => $queried_object,
10.     ]);
11. }
12.
13. if ($is_watched_post_type && $connected->have_posts()) {
14.     ?>
15.         <h3>
```

```
16.          Related <?php echo $queried_object->post_type === 'bookauthor' ?
17.             'Books' : 'Authors' ?>:</h3>
18.     <ul>
19.        <?php while ($connected->have_posts()) : $connected->the_post(); ?>
20.            <li>
21.                <a href="<?php the_permalink(); ?>"><?php the_title(); ?></a>
22.            </li>
23.        <?php endwhile; ?>
24.     </ul>
25.     <?php
26.     wp_reset_postdata();
27. }
```

First, we identify whether the current post being presented is a Book or a Book Author. Once we determine that, we query the available relationships for the current post type. If we get any results, we present a small list of them with the proper link.

As said before, this plugin can do more than that; you can find out more by reading their documentation here[19].

RCCP-Free

The last plugin to take a look at is called RCCP-Free[20]. RCCP stands for RingCentral Communications Plugin. This plugin was written by one of the authors. It incorporates a number of the features of RingCentral's web communications and telephony PHP API. With it, you can place phone calls over the RingCentral embedded phone app, send and receive SMS text messages and emails, and receive call requests from the public side of your WordPress site. You need a free developers account[21] from RingCentral to make this plugin work. You may need a non-free account to use the plugin outside of what is allowed by the free tier.

Once installed, you should see a new admin menu item added like that shown in Figure 9.37. You can access the plugin's settings, add subscribers to your email/SMS distribution list, and list the calls that may have come in while you were away from your admin area.

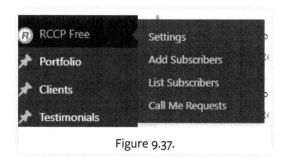

Figure 9.37.

---

[19] documentation here: https://github.com/scribu/wp-posts-to-posts/wiki
[20] RCCP-Free: https://wordpress.org/plugins/rccp-free
[21] free developers account: https://developers.ringcentral.com/free-tier-sign-up.html

Some additional features available with this plugin include:

- RingCentral's embedded phone app can be turned on or off, and calls can be made from within the WordPress Admin area.
- A feature for adding a newsletter (new post) signup widget to the sidebar on the public side of your WordPress installation and asking for both an email address and mobile number as communication channels (double opt-in).
- A feature, based on configuration settings, where you can send out automatic announcements to your collected newsletter list based on their provided (double opt-in) contact information, either email or SMS.
- Adding a Call Me request widget to the sidebar on the public side of your WordPress installation. It allows website visitors to call you using the RingCentral RingOut feature. If no one is online to answer, the request is stored on the admin side.

One of the key features of this plugin is the ability to use and toggle an embedded phone system into your WordPress Admin area. Figure 9.38 shows this part of the plugins settings page with the embedded phone option turned on.

Figure 9.38.

Figure 9.39 shows you what this phone tool looks like when it is turned on. You have to have a valid SSL certificate in place to use the embedded phone.

Figure 9.39.

Chapter

10

Other Resources

We have looked at a significant number of resources in this book, but there are always more added daily. This chapter aims to help you go beyond this book and explore the vast WordPress site development ecosystem. We want to provide the resources to help you answer the questions that have not yet been asked.

The recommended plugins in this book should provide updates regularly, adding features, and improving security. As well, there are always new plugins coming out, so be sure to visit the plugins page often to see what is new. Visit your WordPress sites regularly to make sure they are all up-to-date. Developers may also release new plugins from time to time that can eclipse the plugins we recommend.

Themes

On the subject of themes alone, there is a seemingly endless list on WordPress.org. However, there are other places to find commercial (and therefore unfettered) themes as well. The minimal list is here:

1. **WordPress.org**: https://wordpress.org/themes, provides free themes and plugins; it's the primary location for free WordPress themes. Currently, there are more than 3,800 themes on offer. The themes here are typically lightweight in that they may have some limitations imposed on them in hopes that you like the theme and then buy their pro version. It's not always the case, but be sure to thoroughly vet these themes before you make anything live.

2. **Theme Forest**: https://themeforest.net, sells commercial themes and plugins. Currently, there are over 11,500 different themes available on this site. All of them are commercial, but they vary in pricing, ranging from $13 to $400. The price tends to indicate their worth in terms of WordPress capabilities and features. Look at the live demos of themes that interest you before you make a purchase.

3. **Rocky Themes**: https://rockythemes.com, also sells commercial themes and plugins. They are a single company site that develops two main types of WordPress themes, namely, Creativo and Nimva 3. Each one comes with multiple templates (a theme within a theme), and they are reasonably priced (starting at $59) depending on how many licenses you want. They have great support and a good community of users that help each other with any issues.

4. **Creative Market**: https://creativemarket.com, is another portal for all things commercial WordPress. With over 3,600 themes available for free preview and purchase. There are many plugins here to sift through if you are interested. You can even filter your searches by popularity and age to see what is trending.

Web Resources

This section provides a list of websites where you can find useful resources, tutorials, and tools to build a website. Instead of feeling overwhelmed when facing Google's search box, we want to save you some time and, therefore, money by sending you in the right direction.

We'll look at where to find great themes and plugins not covered in this book. We show you where to find additional written materials and training videos. Then, we discuss conferences that may be worth attending and where to find additional support if you need it. Finally, we share a short description of what to consider to find a reliable web host and list contacts in the WordPress community that are great assets to follow or connect with on twitter.

Written and Visual Materials

Given its longevity, there is a myriad of training and teaching materials on WordPress all over the internet. Blogs are what WordPress was invented for and reciprocally (ironically ?) there are many blogs about WordPress. Here is a list of places that make useful training blogs, articles, courses, image resources, books, and other web resources.

1. **WordPress**: https://wordpress.org/news is both a blog and a support forum. The primary site for WordPress version release and patch news, monthly newsletter, and other technical information. You can also find out about WordCamps near you.

2. **Creative Market**: https://creativemarket.com/blog is a blog with monthly free items. This site has multiple articles per month on design trends and techniques for Word-Press. It covers topics beyond WordPress proper in that there are also articles on web photography, creativity, graphic design, and more.

3. **iThemes**: https://ithemes.com/blog has blog articles on WordPress plugins and techniques. Topics like finding the best popup plugin, the best caching plugins, or the best survey and form building plugins. There is also coverage for security trends, free training webinars, and other educational materials.

4. **O'Reilly Press**: https://oreilly.com has articles, a blog, and books. O'Reilly is a well-known publisher of technical and programming books in multiple disciplines. You can get some excellent WordPress coverage here, but you may have to hunt for it among all the other content.

5. **WP Lift**: https://wplift.com is a blog with guides, interviews, and theme and plugin reviews. This site reviews the latest themes and plugins and covers general WordPress news. It is a useful site for growing your general knowledge of WordPress and its community.

6. **Paletton Color Schemes**: https://paletton.com is a color scheme designer used to find complementary colors. This application is a valuable tool for setting a color theme for your WordPress projects. Given a color HEX code that you or a client wants, you can enter that code, and this tool gives you four complimentary colors with their respective HEX codes.

7. **Unsplash** https://unsplash.com and **Pexels**: https://www.pexels.com offer free, high-resolution images for website use. By using royalty-free, public domain images, you avoid copyright infringement concerns for using images lifted from the web.

8. **GTmetrix**: https://gtmetrix.com provides website speed and performance testing. If you want to ensure your website is operating and serving content as fast as possible, use this web tool to test its speed. You get a comprehensive report on speed and efficiency with a grading scheme. A+ for the best, B for just fair, C- for "See me after class." The report details areas to work on to accelerate page loading, including optimizing images, codebase, and caching.

Conferences

Attending conferences is one of the best ways to make contacts while getting an advanced education. Most WordPress related conferences are called WordCamps, but many other conferences touch on WordPress and blogging in general. Also, there are advanced topics that encompass WordPress' foundational technologies of PHP, MySQL, CSS, and JavaScript. Here are two resources for conferences that we know about, no doubt there are others.

1. **WordCamp Central**, https://central.wordcamp.org, is the central website for finding out when and where the next WordCamp conference will be throughout the world. It's a worthwhile site for WordPress news in general as well.

2. **php[world]**, https://world.phparch.com Although primarily a PHP conference, php[world] is also a great conference to learn about WordPress as well. They pay attention to WordPress topics.

Troubleshooting Assistance

If you need detailed assistance with the WordPress core technology, be sure to visit the documentation and the comprehensive "Codex" area[1]. It looks like the image in Figure 10.1.

There are many pre-made links for you to explore. It includes sections like WordPress basics, working with themes, developing plugins, and even contributing to WordPress itself. Note the list of additional Codex Resources on the right sidebar as well. Each

Figure 10.1.

_____

[1] *"Codex" area: https://codex.wordpress.org/Main_Page*

topic area includes sub-areas you can drill into for further assistance on the issue at hand. For example, if you wanted to know about using plugins, you can see this article of information (Figure 10.2) after clicking on the top-level "Writing a Plugin" link.

Figure 10.2.

If all the above information somehow fails you, then you can always go to the WordPress support forum and ask your question. Only take this step after you have exhausted the FAQ (Frequently asked questions) area and the list of known issues. There is no need to ask the same question 50 times, to be certain, so spend some time trying to figure out your issue on your own first. There is no better feeling of satisfaction after solving your technical problems. However, if you have not found the answer, then be sure to post the question on the forum[2] after you register and login as a member.

Keep in mind that if you are using a commercial theme or plugin, your license typically includes a few months of support that comes along with it. Check with the company or individual behind it for assistance if you have issues with a paid product.

Finding a Great Host

Finding the perfect host to serve your WordPress website(s) is its own specialized skill. Once you find a host you are comfortable with, stay with that host and don't switch to another one at the first sign of trouble. Hosting companies want your business; they can be motivated to fix any issues that come up quickly.

To find an excellent hosting company, keep in mind that there are specific minimum technical requirements for every WordPress site. PHP version 7.3 is now a minimum to look for. Other items to consider are the expected traffic demands for your website and, for media-heavy sites, the amount of disk space available. Therefore, consider if you need a dedicated server or if a shared host can meet your needs. Some may consider the operating system (OS) that the host provides. However, this is generally not an important issue, some prefer a Linux variety as the host OS rather than Apple or Windows, if only because Linux doesn't have licensing costs. If you are maintaining the physical hardware to host your

---

[2] forum: https://wordpress.org/support/forum/how-to-and-troubleshooting

WordPress site, then these items become essential. Since you will be responsible for maintaining, securing, and upgrading the servers, you should explore and understand your needs well in this case.

> NOTE: If you are building WordPress sites for clients as a business, find out if your potential hosting company has an affiliates program. It can give you extra cash for your hosting loyalty.

For further research, see "Finding a Good Host"[3].

The Community

Lastly, we want to draw attention to the WordPress community—the people and companies that support the available products. In addition to all the resources listed earlier in this chapter, there are other places online—like social media—where you can find people and companies talking about WordPress and related topics.

Here is a brief list of Twitter handles we are aware of that you should follow in the WordPress community. This list is not exhaustive, and there are equally as many Facebook and LinkedIn pages, but this should get you started. By following these accounts and checking out who they follow, you can build up more than enough connections to stay current.

- @photomatt—Matt Mullenweg is the creator and leader of the WordPress project.
- @WordPress—the official project account provides updates and news related to WordPress
- @wordcamp—news and information about WordPress events
- @WCEurope—news and info about WordPress events in Europe
- @WordPressTV—tips and tricks for WordPress in video format
- @chrislema—WordPress/WooCommerce evangelist working at liquidweb.com
- @miss_jwo—WordPress Community and Core contributor
- @DavidWolfpaw—WordPress developer working on WordPress core
- @CalEvans—PHP and WordPress developer, conference speaker, and author
- @pbmacintyre—co-author of this book, PHP and WordPress developer, conference speaker
- @lotharthesavior—co-author of this book, PHP and WordPress developer
- @phparch—publisher of books and magazines for PHP and WordPress content

---

[3] "Finding a Good Host": https://phpa.me/wp-finding-host

Index

S

T

U

V

php[architect] Books

The php[architect] series of books cover topics relevant to modern PHP programming. We offer our books in both print and digital formats. Print copy price includes free shipping to the US. Books sold digitally are available to you DRM-free in PDF, ePub, or Mobi formats for viewing on any device that supports these.

To view the complete selection of books and order a copy of your own, please visit: http://phparch.com/books/.

- **The Grumpy Programmer's Guide To Testing PHP Applications (print edition)**
  By Chris Hartjes
  ISBN: 978-1940111797

- **The Fizz Buzz Fix: Secrets to Thinking Like an Experienced Software Developer**
  By Edward Barnard
  ISBN: 978-1940111759

- **The Dev Lead Trenches: Lessons for Managing Developers**
  By Chris Tankersley
  ISBN: 978-1940111711

- **Web Scraping with PHP, 2nd Edition**
  By Matthew Turland
  ISBN: 978-1940111674

- **Security Principles for PHP Applications**
  By Eric Mann
  ISBN: 978-1940111612

- **Docker for Developers, 2nd Edition**
  By Chris Tankersley
  ISBN: 978-1940111568 (Print edition)

- **What's Next? Professional Development Advice**
  Edited by Oscar Merida
  ISBN: 978-1940111513

- **Functional Programing in PHP, 2nd Edition**
  By: Simon Holywell
  ISBN: 978-1940111469

- **Web Security 2016**
  Edited by Oscar Merida
  ISBN: 978-1940111414

- **Integrating Web Services with OAuth and PHP**
  By Matthew Frost
  ISBN: 978-1940111261

10. Index

- **Zend Framework 1 to 2 Migration Guide**
  By Bart McLeod
  ISBN: 978-1940111216

- **XML Parsing with PHP**
  By John M. Stokes
  ISBN: 978-1940111162

- **Zend PHP 5 Certification Study Guide, Third Edition**
  By Davey Shafik with Ben Ramsey
  ISBN: 978-1940111100

- **Mastering the SPL Library**
  By Joshua Thijssen
  ISBN: 978-1940111001

Feedback and Updates

Please let us know what you thought of this book! What did you enjoy? What was confusing or could have been improved? Did you find errata? Any feedback and thoughts you have regarding this book will help us improve a future edition.

To leave a review, go to https://phpa.me/wpdevdepth-book

Updates

To keep in touch and be notified about future editions to this book, visit http://phparch.com and sign up for our (low-volume) mailing list.

You can also follow us on twitter @phparch and on facebook: https://facebook.com/phparch/